D1000785
GOLDEN
ARROW
PENSHURST

BULLEID PACIFICS AT WORK

Below: No 35014 *Nederland Line* puts up an impressive smokescreen, with the 09.15 Waterloo-Exeter near Basingstoke, illustrating the fact that in bad conditions a driver's view could be completely obscured. *R. E. Wilson*

BULLEID PACIFICS AT WORK

Colonel H.C.B. Rogers OBE

LONDON
IAN ALLAN LTD

TO MY WIFE
who saw glamour depart
with
The Southern Pacifics

First published 1980

ISBN 0 7110 1074 9

Published by Ian Allan Ltd, Shepperton, Surrey; and printed by Ian Allan Printing Ltd at their works at Coombelands in Runnymede, England

Contents

Acknowledgements

In some respects this book is a sequel to *The Bulleid Pacifics of the Southern* by Cecil J. Allen and S. C. Townroe (London, Ian Allan Ltd, 1951, reprinted 1976), but it contains much which could not, for various reasons, have been included in that earlier work. I have had so much generous assistance, indeed, from Mr S. C. Townroe, CEng, FIMechE, that without it my contribution to the history of the Bulleid Pacifics would be very slim indeed. Mr C. P. Atkins, Librarian at the National Railway Museum, York, has also helped me much with my research, particularly by finding for me correspondence and reports from the files of the Eastleigh Locomotive Works. I am indebted, too, to my friends Mr R. A. Riddles, CBE, FIMechE and Mr R. C. Bond, FICE, FIMechE, for information and comments; and to Mr H. A. V. Bulleid, FIMechE for his reminiscences of his brilliant father. Finally, MR R. G. Jarvis, FIMechE has told me a lot about his rebuilding of the two classes of Pacifics.

Left: On 28 November 1964 No 34018 *Axminster* pulls a down Bournemouth train away from Basingstoke. *J. B. Wells*

1
The background

At a meeting of the Southern Railway Board in May 1937, the Chairman, Mr (later Sir Robert) Holland-Martin, announced that the Chief Mechanical Engineer, R. E. L. Maunsell, who had been suffering from ill health, would be retiring on 31 October and that he would be succeeded by O. V. S. Bulleid from the London & North Eastern Railway.

Maunsell had been one of the most able CMEs of modern times. Though handicapped by the concentration of resources on the progressive electrification of the Southern Railway, he had provided the company with a very competent stud of modern steam locomotives. Before the Grouping of the railways in 1923, Maunsell had been Chief Mechanical Engineer of the South Eastern & Chatham Railway for the preceding 10 years, and before that he had held the same appointment on the Great Southern & Western Railway of Ireland.

Locomotive and carriage affairs on the SE&CR were not in a very satisfactory state when Maunsell accepted the offer to become its CME, and he soon started selecting a staff from other railways whom he felt had the knowledge and drive to achieve the results he wanted. He had been impressed with G. J. Churchward's work on the Great Western Railway, and so from Swindon came G. H. Pearson as Assistant CME and Works Manager at Ashford, L. Lynes as Leading Carriage & Wagon Draughtsman, and H. Holcroft to plan the extension and reorganisation of the Ashford Locomotive, Carriage and Wagon Shops. From the Midland Railway, Maunsell recruited the very able J. Clayton to be Chief Draughtsman and later Personal Assistant to the CME. Pearson's influence led to much of Great Western practice, including long-travel, long-lap valves, being incorporated in all subsequent SE&CR designs for new and rebuilt locomotives; whereas Clayton's hand can be seen in the close exterior resemblance of the rebuilt 'D' and 'E' class 4-4-0s to the Midland Class 2s (though they far from resembled these rather sluggish engines in performance!)

On the formation of the Southern Railway in 1923, Maunsell was appointed CME and the members of his staff noted above accompanied him to Waterloo, retaining their previous positions except that Holcroft became Technical Assistant to the CME. It was clear, therefore, that Ashford practice was to dominate new locomotive design policy.

This book is concerned primarily, of course, with Bulleid's Pacific locomotives; but before considering them it is necessary to discuss the engines of Maunsell's design which they were intended to displace.

In 1917 Maunsell's team had copied the Great Western in producing a mixed traffic two-cylinder 2-6-0 with taper boiler, long-lap, long-travel valves, high pressure and top feed; but had improved on Swindon practice by adopting a higher degree of superheat. The performance and ability of this locomotive was such that the Government chose the type when they decided to build general-purpose locomotives at Woolwich Arsenal to alleviate the unemployment distress which followed the reduction of the Arsenal's activities after the end of World War 1. The Southern Railway eventually possessed 80 of these locomotives, of which 50 were built at Woolwich (and known by SR locomotive men as the 'Woolworths'). They were called the 'N' class on the SE&CR and SR. Six additional engines, the 'N1' class, were built with three-cylinders so that, with the smaller outside cylinders, they could work over the Hastings line with its restricted loading gauge.

Of very similar design to the 'Ns' were the 'U' class engines with 6ft coupled wheels instead of 5ft 6in. The first of these had been built originally as 2-6-4 passenger tank engines, but after an accident they were considered as being too unsteady at high speeds on some of the less well constructed secondary routes and were converted to tender engines. As such they were very successful; many more were built for passenger traffic on secondary lines and the class eventually numbered 50. As in the case of the 'Ns', there was a three-cylinder version, the 'U1' class, of 21 locomotives.

The boilers and most other details of these 2-6-0s were identical. For the purposes for which they were intended, the Maunsell Moguls were some of the most satisfactory locomotives to run in the British Isles. The Midland Great Western Railway of Ireland bought 20 of the Woolwich-built engines, and, after the amalgamations, the Great Southern Railways bought six more, but gave them 6ft wheels and so made them equivalent to the 'U' class. The Metropolitan Railway also bought some of the 2-6-4T type.

On the formation of the Southern Railway, however, there were not enough locomotives powerful enough to deal with the heavy express traffic envisaged, let alone to improve the schedules; for in October 1923, some 10 months after the Grouping, the Traffic Manager stated a requirement for 20 express engines capable of working 500 ton trains at an average speed of 55mph. Clayton and Holcroft discussed the types that would be suitable to meet this requirement. Clayton favoured a four-cylinder 4-6-0 with a narrow firebox, believing that this would be cheaper to run than a Pacific and arguing that a wide grate was not necessary on account of the Southern Railway's comparatively short runs. Holcroft, with his Great Western experience, agreed, but suggested the advantages of a crank setting of 135°, instead of the normal 180°, and giving eight exhausts per revolution instead of four resulting in a more even turning moment. A Drummond four-cylinder 4-6-0, No 449, was accordingly tried out with this setting and showed a 10% saving in coal per ton-mile. Before making a firm recommendation to Maunsell, Clayton had trips on a Great Western 'Castle' and a LNER Pacific. These confirmed the opinion at which he and Holcroft had arrived.[1]

Maunsell agreed to this proposal, but it would obviously be some time before a fleet of the new locomotives could be in operation, and by March 1924 the need for heavy express passenger engines on the Western Section (the old LSWR) had become urgent. The latest LSWR express locomotives were Urie's two-cylinder 4-6-0s of the 'N15' class. They had not, however, proved entirely satisfactory in service because their steam pressure could not be reliably maintained. Nevertheless, Maunsell believed that they were potentially very good engines, for they embodied many of the good points which, from his long experience, he had adopted in his own designs. They were built for strength and durability; with their outside Walschaerts valve gear and high running plate, everything was accessible; the bearings were of generous dimensions; and lubrication of cylinders, valves, and axleboxes were provided from the footplate where the enginemen could get at it. Furthermore, they had plenty of power and a well-tried type of boiler. To try and find out the cause of the steaming trouble, Maunsell had tests carried out with No 742 of the class. The steam ports were enlarged and the exhaust release point set a little earlier to sharpen the blast; but these measures effected no improvement. Urie had fitted stovepipe chimneys with a comparatively small diameter to all his 4-6-0s except the first of them, the 'H15' mixed traffic engine, under the impression that the exhaust would thereby escape with considerable velocity and so carry the smoke and steam above the level of the cab windows. The stovepipe chimney on No 742 was now replaced by the larger lipped variety of the 'H15' class, together with its larger petticoat pipe. This enabled the blastpipe cap to be enlarged from 5in dia to 5⅛in. A trial run after these alterations had been carried out showed a greatly improved performance, with the steaming much more consistent and an increase in the maximum indicated horsepower from 950 to 1,250. (The 'H15' chimney, with minor alterations and the addition of a capuchon, was subsequently adopted for the 'Arthurs', 'Nelsons' and 'Schools'.)

Urie had been rebuilding some of Drummond's four-cylinder 4-6-0s as 'H15' mixed traffic engines, and 10 more were awaiting conversion. The Running Department, however, did not want any more of them for mixed traffic and asked if they could be rebuilt with larger wheels for passenger work. In the light of the experiments with No 742 and in order to get some powerful express engines quickly, Maunsell decided to rebuild completely these 10 engines, Nos 448-457, as 'Ashfordised' 'N15s'; that is to say, with long-lap valves having a travel of 6$^{9}/_{16}$in, a boiler pressure of 200lb/sq in instead of 180, main steam pipes following a direct path to the valve chests, slightly smaller diameter cylinders, and the Maunsell superheater. These were, of course, virtually new engines. On test No 451 showed itself capable of maintaining 1500ihp. In due course the Urie 'N15s' were modified in the same fashion as No 742 and were all fitted with the Maunsell superheater and smaller cylinders, but they retained their short travel valves.[2]

Eventually there were 54 of the excellent Maunsell 'N15s', built during 1925 and 1926. They were all named after King Arthur and his Knights of the Round Table, while the Urie 'N15s' were given other names from the Arthurian legends. Apart from traffic on the Western Section, they took over the principal London to Dover and Folkestone trains on 1 July 1925; the permissible load being raised from the 300 tons handled by the 'E1' and 'D1' rebuilds to 425 tons. At the time these services were particularly difficult to work. Because of the very frequent electric trains between London and as far out as Orpington, the speed of the boat trains was limited to that of the stopping electrics. After clearing this section the troubles were not over because there was immediately the three-mile climb to Knockholt summit and a number of speed restrictions after that. Even with the 'King Arthurs' the best possible timing with the 425 ton trains was 103min for the 78 miles, or 45.4mph.[3]

In August 1926 Holcroft rode on the first of the four-cylinder 4-6-0s, No E850 *Lord Nelson*, during its trial runs. The boiler of the new engine was based on that of the Maunsell Moguls, but enlarged to the limit of the SR composite loading gauge. The grate area of 33sq ft was larger than that of any other existing British 4-6-0 (though exceeded by that of the Great Western 'King' class 4-6-0 of the following year). To achieve this large area in a narrow firebox, its length was 10ft 6in with the front half sloping more than the back. Although this was only 18in longer than the 'King Arthur' firebox, the extra distance of the front firebars from the firehole demanded a lot more skill in the use of the shovel. If the fireman was unable to shoot shovelfuls of coal on to the front firebars, the unfed area of the grate would burn thin, allowing a large volume of cold air to be drawn in, and the coal which fell short of this area would form a ridge across the middle of the grate, making it even more difficult to cast the full length. As a result there would be a rapid fall in the steam pressure. To try and correct this, the fireman would seize a long fire iron with which to spread the fire more evenly over the grate. But this is not an easy tool to manipulate at speed.[4]

Only 16 'Nelsons' were built and, owing to the necessity of their being manned by crews skilled in driving and firing them, they were allocated during their lifetime to only four depots. Until 1939, indeed, they were divided between only two, Nine Elms and Stewarts Lane; but after that Eastleigh and Bournemouth got some as well; but from 1948 all were at one depot, Eastleigh. If the firing was good and the boilers carefully maintained, the 'Nelsons' were excellent and could work easily the most exacting schedules on the Southern.[5]

After initial 'teething' troubles, Holcroft had two remarkably high speed runs with E850 between Waterloo and Salisbury and back with the 'Atlantic Coast Express'. The engine was thoroughly tried out for two years before Maunsell ordered any more, because he was determined that any faults should be found and put right rather than incur the expense of modifying a complete batch. In fact no alterations were needed, and during 1928 and 1929 another 10 Nelsons were built. Subsequently 15 more were requested, but Sir Herbert Walker, the General Manager, reduced the figure to 5. This was a mistake because the 'Nelsons' were divided between the Eastern and Western Sections, and there were thus insufficient to form 'Nelson' links, so that trains had to be of a weight which an 'Arthur' could tackle if a 'Nelson' was not available. Holcroft writes: 'The "Nelsons" were perhaps the most reliable, trouble free, and economical in many ways of all the Southern locomotives, but in performance I think they could have been better.'[6]

On 17 August 1937 Holcroft had his last trip on a 'Nelson', No 862 *Lord Collingwood*, which had the Kylchap exhaust and double chimney. He writes: 'I was most favourably impressed by the performance of this engine. It was very lively and free running; despite the numerous signal checks up to Sevenoaks, time lost by each was quickly recovered . . . I noticed that the right-hand side of the sloping part of the grate received more coal than the left, but that the left-hand side of the shorter horizontal part received more in the back corner than the right. This rather suggested that the blastpipe and chimney setting was slightly at fault'.[7] (This observation of Holcroft's is of interest in the light of subsequent claims that 'Nelsons' fitted with the Lemaître exhaust were more economical than *Lord Collingwood*.) Although the Locomotive Running Department gave a favourable report on the Kylchap device, nothing more was done about it at the time.

The 'Nelsons' and 'Arthurs' met most of the Southern's current traffic needs, but neither class could work over the Tonbridge-St Leonards line which carried the important express services between London and Hastings. Passenger stock for this line was built with 6in less width than the normal coaches because of the restricted loading gauge which altogether with numerous sharp curves and the under-sized Mountfield Tunnel, caused considerable operating problems. Locomotives were needed that could haul the Charing Cross-Hastings trains to the same timings between London and Tonbridge, and with similar loads, as were worked by the 'Arthurs' on the trains between London and the Kentish coast. The tractive effort would therefore have to be similar, but it could not be obtained with two outside cylinders because their size would have been too great for the loading gauge. A multi-cylinder engine was therefore needed; but six coupled wheels were ruled out because, with a leading bogie, the overall length and consequent 'throw-over' would have been too much for the line's sharp curves. The ingenious solution was a 'three-quarter Nelson' with three cylinders (the two outside ones being identical with the 'Nelson's'). There were four-coupled 'Nelson' wheels as well as 'Nelson' motion parts and other items. As the cab had to be reduced in width over the cornices a Belpaire firebox presented difficulties, so a shortened 'Arthur' boiler, with its round-topped firebox, was chosen. These engines, named after public schools and known as the 'Schools', or 'V' class, were outstandingly successful and were probably the finest 4-4-0s ever built anywhere. The tractive effort was about the same as the 'Arthurs', but they weighed one coach less, and they could rival the 'Arthurs' in performance. When the 'Schools' first appeared the Hastings route was not ready for them and they were soon demonstrating their prowess on the Eastern and Western Section main lines.[8]

Holcroft called the 40 'Schools' 'the best value for money ever put on rails'. He says that at a pinch they could tackle jobs usually allotted to 'Nelsons' and that they could exceed the hauling power of the 'Arthurs'.[9] One of these engines is perhaps unique, for No 902 *Wellington* figures in one of the stained glass windows of Wellington College chapel.

Notes

1 Holcroft, H.: *Locomotive Adventure*; London, Ian Allan Ltd, pp119, 120
2 Townroe, S. C.; *The Arthurs, Nelsons and Schools of the Southern*; London, Ian Allan Ltd, 1973, pp33-4, 39-43
3 Holcroft, *op cit*, pp134, 147
4 Townroe, *op cit*, pp46-8
5 *ibid*
6 Holcroft, *op cit*, pp136-9, 148, 152
7 Holcroft, H.; *Locomotive Adventure* Vol II; London, Ian Allan Ltd, 1965, pp263-4
8 Townroe, *op cit*, pp57-62
9 Holcroft; Vol II, *op cit*, pp274-5, 278

Below: Before Bulleid introduced his Pacific designs the Southern's 'modern' top link motive power was mainly provided by two 4-6-0 classes and one 4-4-0. 'Lord Nelson' No 30859 *Lord Hood* is seen in postwar Southern days, with Bulleid's Lemaitre type chimney/blastpipe arrangement and redesigned cylinders. All 16 of the class were so rebuilt.
Eric Treacy

Above right: The main stay of the express locomotive stock, the 'King Arthur' class. No E763 *Sir Bors de Ganis* is seen in early Southern days before the fitting of smoke deflectors. *IAL*

Right: Possibly the best known of the 4-4-0 wheel arrangement was the 'Schools' class. No 901 *Winchester* in Hildenborough cutting with a Hastings-London express, has acquired the Lemaitre blastpipe/chimney arrangement. Of the 40 engines, only 21 were so modified as unlike the 'Lord Nelsons' little improvement in performance was attained.
Eric Treacy

SOUTHERN
763

SOUTHERN
901
421

2
The new CME

On 20 September 1937 O. V. S. Bulleid arrived at Waterloo to start understudying Maunsell prior to taking over. It was an interesting period in locomotive design, due particularly to the marked advance that had been made in boiler construction. By the end of the 1920s locomotive engineers were designing boilers which would allow higher pressures and temperatures without incurring maintenance troubles. They had also learned, primarily from the work of André Chapelon, the value of direct and wide steam passages from the superheater, through the admission and exhaust ports to the blastpipe.

Their attention was then logically drawn to possible improvements in the blastpipe, which was still normally the single simple nozzle, with the twin aims of reducing the back pressure and improving the gas flow through the boiler.

Another development which excited their interest was the poppet valve, which seemed to offer better control of the admission of steam into, and its exhaust from, the cylinders, as compared with the piston valve. With the latter the timings of admission and exhaust were permanently linked; but by using poppet valves the timing of both events could be varied independently of one another. Trials with poppet valves continued until the end of steam traction, and though by that time they had not demonstrated such superiority as to justify their extra cost and complication, British Railways Class 5 4-6-0s fitted with Caprotti poppet valve gear showed a significant reduction in coal consumption and maintenance costs. Nevertheless, piston valves could be improved considerably by increasing their diameter, as was shown by Bulleid with his alterations to the 'Lord Nelsons'.

Improvements in the boiler and steam circuit were not, however, the only aspects of the steam locomotive that were receiving attention. Much was being done to raise standards of reliability, particularly in those components most likely to suffer from increases in power output. A great deal of thought was devoted to inside big-ends, coupled axleboxes, coupling rods, and pistons — all of which were prone to sudden disintegration or rapid wear at speed.

On the LNER, Bulleid had been Principal Assistant to Sir Nigel Gresley and had been closely associated with the development of Gresley's latest express passenger locomotives: the 'P2' class 2-8-2s and the 'A4' class Pacifics. In addition, over a period of several years, he had had contacts with the famous French locomotive engineer, André Chapelon.

Gresley had been impressed with Chapelon's work at the time the latter had been in the Research & Development Section of the Paris-Orléans Railway. In 1926 Chapelon designed his Kylchap exhaust, the object of which was to produce an adequate draught over the whole smokebox and to mix the gases with the exhaust steam so thoroughly that the mixture might be expelled with the minimum of effort. Trials of this exhaust on the Paris-Orléans gave such remarkable results that in 1928 Gresley obtained drawings of it so that he could try the device himself. By October of that year one of the LNER 'Shire' or 'D49' class 4-4-0s, No 251 *Derbyshire,* had been fitted in Darlington Works with a Kylchap exhaust. First reports were good, and in January 1929 Darlington was instructed to fit a similar exhaust to No 322 *Huntingdonshire,* which had Lentz OC poppet valves. The latter engine was ready in April 1929. In the meantime Chapelon had visited England at Gresley's invitation and had ridden on the footplate of *Derbyshire* from Kings Cross to York. The engine ran quite well, but Chapelon saw that it was not steaming as well as it should. He discovered that sundry errors had been made in fitting the Kychap exhaust, and told Gresley. In 1930 these exhausts were removed from both engines, but that the trials had been valuable is shown by the subsequent adoption of the Kylchap system by Gresley and his two successors.[1]

Also in 1929 there was completed at Darlington Works Gresley's four-cylinder compound 4-6-4 locomotive No 10000 with a Yarrow water-tube boiler and a pressure of 450lb/sq in. It did not, however, come up to expectations. It proved difficult to keep the boiler walls airtight, and acceleration was weak when working compound after a stop, owing to the time taken to build up the superheat. After a year or two of trials both Gresley and Bulleid had discussions with Chapelon as to what could be done to improve the engine. Chapelon pointed out that the degree of superheat was insufficient to avoid condensation in the low-pressure cylinders and that it should be increased. He added that even better results could be obtained by re-superheating between the high and low-pressure cylinders, and that the fitting of a Kylchap exhaust would help. In May 1935, therefore, No 10000 received a double Kylchap exhaust and re-superheat. Performance and efficiency were improved considerably, but the lack of air-tightness remained a problem. In 1937 the engine was rebuilt as a conventional three-cylinder simple with a conventional boiler.[2]

Meanwhile, in November 1929 Chapelon's revolutionary rebuild of a P-O Pacific, No 3566, was turned out from the Company's Tours Works. Gresley was so interested in its astonishing performance that he sent Bullied to Tours to watch some of the trials. The result of Bulleid's observations was that Gresley embodied some features of Chapelon's practice in his 2-8-2 locomotive, No 2001 *Cock o' the North,* which was built in 1934. Of its design Gresley, in his second Presidential Address to the Institution of Locomotive Engineers, said: 'I did not hesitate to incorporate some of the outstanding features of the Paris-Orléans Railway engines, such as the provision of extra-large steam passages and a double blastpipe. There was no real novelty in these features but the French engineers had worked out the designs scientifically and had proved them by the results obtained in actual service.' This statement was not, in fact, quite correct, because the double blastpipe included the Kylchap pattern exhaust, which was undoubtedly a novelty.

At Gresley's request arrangements were made for *Cock o' the North* to be tried on the Vitry test plant. The engine ran to Harwich in December 1934, pulling some 40 ton wagons loaded with the coal with which it was normally fired. From there they were all shipped to Calais, and ran over the French railways to Vitry-sur-Seine, where Bulleid arrived to watch the tests. These were disappointing, because, like many other engines, *Cock o' the North* could not be driven hard on the test plant without the axles overheating. Gresley thereupon visited Chapelon to ask him what should be done. Chapelon proposed a trial on the line with a test load. This trial duly took place on the P-O between Les Aubrais and Tours, and was quite satisfactory. Bulleid, indeed, claimed in a discussion at the Institution of Locomotive Engineers in 1947 that the engine was extremely efficient on the testing plant and compared favourably with the French engines in her coal consumption per rail-hp, and better still per dbhp. When tested on the open road between Orléans and Tours, she developed, he said, 'a very high horsepower of the order of 2,800, and again showed herself to be an efficient engine from the point of view of coal consumption per dbhp.' Bulleid was speaking some 13 years after the trials and his memory of events was a little inaccurate.

In a letter to the author, Chapelon said that *Cock o' the North* was tested on the open road against one of his own Pacifics, with the following results:

	Cock o' the North	P-O Pacific	
Speed	68mph	68mph	56mph
dbhp	1,910	1,910	2,700
Water per hp/hr	10.45kg	7.5kg	8.20kg
Coal per hp/hr	1.48kg	1.05kg	1.22kg

These figures show that the P-O Pacific was far superior to the LNER engine. Gresley, at any rate, had no illusions; for he told the Institution of Locomotive Engineers that the first *Cock o' the North* would be the last and that any subsequent 'P2' class engines would embody the lessons learned in France. The second of the class, *Earl Marischal,* was completed in October 1934, before the despatch of *Cock o' the North* to France, and differed from the latter in having Walschaerts valve gear instead of Lentz poppet valves. In 1936 four more of the 'P2' class were built, and these had larger steam passages, as well as the double Kylchap exhaust. The lessons of the French trials had already been incorporated in the 'A4' Pacifics, the first of which appeared in September 1935. These early 'A4s' did not have the double Kylchap exhaust, but the batch of 1938 had it, and one of these, *Mallard,* achieved the world record for steam traction of 126mph.

Bulleid arrived, therefore, on the Southern Railway with a wide knowledge of the best French practice, and that he had absorbed Chapelon's teaching on the steam circuit was to be evident in his own designs.

The locomotives of the Maunsell regime had, as has been said, met the traffic needs for which they had been designed; but by 1937 some of the services were stretching their abilities, particularly on the heavy Dover and Folkestone boat expresses. The 'Nelsons' could manage them, but only just. The difficulty lay principally in the increased density of the suburban electric services which entailed much slow running before the express got clear of the London area; and the 'Nelsons' lacked sufficient acceleration to make good any delays incurred when working such heavy trains as the 460ton Pullman 'Golden Arrow' over this difficult route. The 'Night Ferry', indeed, with its massive *Wagons-Lits* coaches, had to be double-headed, normally with two 4-4-0s. There was a clear need, therefore, for a more powerful express locomotive, but it would not be possible to produce one before 1940; so Bulleid sought means of improving the capacity of the 'Nelsons' as a temporary measure.

Soon after he took over, Bulleid began making numerous footplate trips, to find out for himself what the Maunsell engines were like. An obvious early selection, in the light of his LNER experience, was No 862 *Lord Collingwood,* with its 1K/1C pattern double Kylchap exhaust. On his instructions, the engine was driven in full gear up Grosvenor Road bank out of Victoria, and then at 40-50% cut-off for the rest of the way to Dover. Along the straight, between Tonbridge and Ashford, the regulator was kept wide open and both injectors working to keep the water level in sight in the water gauges. Speeds were between 90 and 95mph, and when the engine reached Dover the fireman was exhausted, but Bulleid was delighted.[3]

It was evidently clear to Bulleid from this experience that an improved exhaust was one of the measures that were worth applying to the 'Nelsons'. The Southern had also bought a double Kylchap of Chapelon's other pattern, the 1K/T. In both types the exhaust steam, after leaving the top of the standpipe leading from the cylinders, passed through a conical blastpipe nozzle fitted with four radial wedge-shaped inserts. These inserts divided the steam into four jets which, drawing some of the exhaust gases with them, passed into the four lobes of the Kylala spreader, which was mounted a short distance above. The division of the exhaust steam into four jets improved still further the entrainment of the hot gases above the exit from these lobes where more of the hot gases circulated. In the 1K/1C (ie 1 Kylala and 1 *cylindre,* or petticoat) the mixture was then carried through a petticoat to a final mixing with the remainder of the gases and out through the chimney. In the 1K/T (ie 1 Kylala and a *trompe* or trumpet) the final mixing was dispensed with, and instead of the petticoat, there was a downward extension of the chimney, swelling out in diameter. Bulleid had the 1K/T fitted to No 865 *Sir John Hawkins.* The Northern Railway of France used a variant of the Kylchap 1K/T in which the chimney with its trumpet extension, though of a much larger diameter, was retained, and the Kylala spreader with its four lobes was replaced by a fitting, which was also multiple but which had six jets, of which five were fixed in a circle and the sixth was in the centre and could be adjusted from closed to fully open. It was a good system, but, as Chapelon says,[4] it suffered from the disadvantage of not functioning as a mixer; and its characteristic curve was inferior to that of the Kylchap.[5] However, it had the virtue of simplicity, it was not covered by a patent, and it could be made in the Southern's own works. Bulleid fitted this, together with a large diameter chimney, to No 863 *Lord Rodney;* but he decided to simplify it further by omitting the central variable jet. Trials between the three engines were not exhaustive enough to be conclusive, but Bullied apparently decided that his modified Lemaître was adequate for his purpose.

Because the 'Nelsons' performed considerably better with an improved exhaust system, the Lemaître and large chimney were fitted to all of them. In addition Bulleid introduced Chapelon features by directing Eastleigh to design new cylinders with 10in dia piston valves, in place of the original ones of 8in dia, together with improved steam and exhaust passages. This modification was gradually applied to all the 'Nelsons' except Nos 851 and 863.[6] With their new steam circuit, the 'Nelsons' were excellent engines, which could meet all the needs of the Eastern Section for the time being.

Following his success with the 'Nelsons', Bulleid fitted a number of the 'Urie Arthurs' with the modified Lemaître exhaust. These rather undistinguished engines had generally been used on semi-fast services and on Southampton boat trains, van trains, and specials. Until electrification they also worked passenger trains on the Portsmouth direct line.[7] Equipped with the Lemaître system, they were much better, even though retaining their short-travel valves. Encouraged by this, Bulleid modified half the 'Schools' in similar fashion; but these outstanding engines were already so good that there appeared to be little difference in their performance, and the intended fitting of the Lemaître to the other 20 engines was therefore cancelled.[8] It is a pity that trials were not carried out before the first 20 were modified, because the large chimney, whilst reasonably acceptable on the 'Nelsons', ruined the looks of the handsome 'Schools'.

In connection with the 'Schools', Holcroft suggested to Bulleid that counter-balancing reciprocating parts on a three-cylinder locomotive was quite unnecessary because the longitudinal forces were self-balanced and the weight was only added to offset the couples set up by the forces working in different planes. If all reciprocating balance were omitted it would result in the abolition of hammer blow on the rails. He proposed that this theory should be tried out one of the 'Schools'. Bulleid accepted this and the balance weights on one of the class were cut down so that they balanced rotating parts only. The Locomotive Testing Section reported that the riding was no different from others of the class and that wear, after a period, was unaffected. No more engines were altered, but the experiment resulted in all reciprocating balance being omitted from Bulleid's Pacifics, with consequent absence of hammer blow.[9]

The subsequent history of the two Kylchap exhaust assemblies purchased by the Southern Railway is something of a mystery. It appears that they were sold to the LNER, who put them into store. Some time later two Kylchaps (it is thought the same two) turned up at Derby. The 1K/1C assembly was put on the LMS 'Duchess' class Pacific No 6245 *City of London*. This came to light when somebody asked why this engine was making a different noise to the others of its class. It was removed again at some date unknown. The 1K/T assembly was fitted to one of the two double-chimney 'Jubilee' class engines, either No 5684 *Jutland*, or No 5742 *Connaught*, which retained it until the locomotive was scrapped.[10]

Notes

1 Chapelon, A.: information to the Author
Rogers, Colonel H. C. B.: *Thompson & Peppercorn: Locomotive Engineers*, London, Ian Allan Ltd, 1979, pp.37-8
2 *ibid*, pp41-2
Chapelon, A.: information to the Author
3 Townroe, S. C.: *The Arthurs, Nelsons and Schools of the Southern;* London, Ian Allan Ltd, 1973, p55
4 Chapelon, A.: *La Locomotive à Vapeur*, 2nd edn, Vol I; J. B. Ballière et Fils, Paris, 1952, p135
5 *ibid*, p136
6 Townroe, *op cit*, p55
7 *ibid*, pp83-4
8 Holcroft, H.: *Locomotive Adventure*, Vol II; London, Ian Allan Ltd, 1965, pp274-9
9 *ibid*
10 Townend, P. N. and Carpenter, G. W.: information to the Author.

Above left: O. V. S. Bulleid, facing camera. *S. C. Townroe*

Left: Gresley Class W1 4-6-4 No 10000. *IAL*

Below: Gresley Class P2 2-8-2 No 2002 *Earl Marischal*. *IAL*

3
The design of the 'Merchant Navy' Pacifics

It is possible that O. V. S. Bulleid's Pacific locomotives have fascinated more locomotive enthusiasts than have any other steam engines of more recent years; certainly the records of the National Railway Museum suggest that they have been the subject of the most enquiries. It may be that the reason for this lies in their scintillating performance when at their best, contrasted with the appalling maintenance problems presented by some of the more unorthodox features of their design. When Bulleid's engines were rebuilt to retain their best features and discard those that had caused trouble, they became equal in all respects to the best of their type and power class in the country. Yet, paradoxically, many (but not those who had to maintain them when in their original form) lamented their transformation, believing that some sparkle in prowess had been lost. Certainly Bulleid himself, a very sensitive man, was profoundly distressed at their rebuilding.[1] Nevertheless, their achievements in their final form owed as much to the talent of their original designer as to the skill of those who modified his work.

At the time of Bulleid's appointment as CME of the Southern Railway, the chairman was R. Holland-Martin. He had been appointed a Director on the Board of the London & South Western Railway in 1910, and had continued as such when the LSWR became the predominant partner in the amalgamations of 1923 which produced the Southern Railway. He was also a Director, and later Chairman, of Martins Bank, and his particular value to the Railway was as a financial adviser. However, he called himself a railwayman and devoted some of his time to travelling around the system and meeting the staff at work. At the end of 1934 he succeeded Lord Wakehurst as Chairman of the Southern Railway. He was always full of ideas for developing and improving what he regarded as the 'Southern Service' to the public, and he had backed whole-heartedly the Company's vast electrification schemes. Popularly known as 'RHM', he had the same kind of fertile and volatile mind as Bulleid, and was therefore likely to be receptive to the latter's flights of imaginative ideas. It was, perhaps, an unfortunate combination, because Bulleid needed a cautious restraining hand until these ideas had been fully tried out in practice.

Bulleid had sound theoretical reasons for all the features embodied in the design of his locomotives, but like many people of inventive thought, once he had designed anything he appeared to lose interest in it and to become absorbed in other matters that engaged his attention. These could be anything from locomotives and coaches to the design of Eastleigh Works gates or the use of old wagon headstocks to cut up into ornamental panelling. He was never interested in conducting lengthy experiments to ascertain whether novelty in design would or would not contribute to increased efficiency or reliability, or whether some modification was needed in the light of practical results. He was in some respects not unlike Field-Marshal Viscount Montgomery, who expected his staff to deal with the current battle whilst he was busy preparing for the next one. Thus Bulleid, who took it for granted that his new ideas would work, found it hard to listen patiently to difficulties presented by his staff, though trade representatives with some novelty to sell found him a willing audience and an eager purchaser if their wares promised to further his projects; hence the steam-operated fire doors, patent water gauges, phosphorescent gauge dials, decorative enamelled nameplates, and so on.[2] J. F. Harrison, who knew him well on the LNER, says that the extra cost of any fitting would not have deterred Bulleid, adding that: 'If it was made of gold and he wanted it, he would have it.'[3] On the LNER his unconventional outlook on locomotives horrified A. H. Peppercorn, to whom he is said to have remarked: 'Pepp, if you design a locomotive with five driving wheels, your name is made.'[4]

The immediate problem facing the new CME was the design of an engine that would have the tractive effort and boiler capacity to meet the increasing demands of the steam-worked traffic without exceeding the main line axle-load limit of 21 tons or the restrictions imposed by the Southern Railway composite loading gauge. It was a problem which excited little enthusiasm among most members of the Board of a railway that was pressing ever onwards with electrification. Yet there had been no design for a heavy express locomotive since the insufficient 'Lord Nelson' class of 1926, and it would be many years before electrification could oust steam from all the main lines. This was well understood by 'RHM', so that Board approval was eventually obtained, with little difficulty. On 2 March 1938, therefore, the Rolling Stock Committee of the Board authorised the construction of 10 new main line steam engines, but omitted any mention as to their type. Bulleid at this stage kept his thoughts and plans very much to himself, and indeed there is no record of affairs between that date and the start of construction at Eastleigh in 1939.[5]

Bulleid believed that his engines must be capable of hauling trains of from 550 to 600 tons weight on the Western Section at 70mph and the Continental boat trains on the Eastern Section at 60mph. By comparison, 'King Arthurs' were limited to trains of 11 coaches on Western Section express timings, and the difficulties with the boat trains have already been mentioned. He thought first of a 4-8-2 type, but he found that this would be too long for the existing turntables. Then he considered a 2-8-2, probably in the light of his experiences with the LNER 'P2' class, but the Civil Engineer did not favour pony trucks on engines hauling express trains because of the disastrous accident at Sevenoaks to an express headed by a 2-6-4T engine. A trailing truck was essential because Bulleid wanted a wide firebox; he therefore offered a Pacific, which the Civil Engineer accepted.[6]

Bulleid's eagerness to see his locomotives on the road had some unfortunate results. S. C. Townroe recalls that he never discussed with his own Chief, the Locomotive Running Superintendent, the kind of engines that were needed nor did he seek any advice about practical running matters. The facilities available at running sheds were therefore not studied, and one result was that the height of their tenders prevented the Pacifics from being coaled at the Eastleigh and Salisbury stages until special conveyors were hastily installed. Bulleid used the design team in the Eastleigh Works drawing office, but, as he regarded the Chief Draughtsman as too cautious, he replaced him by C. S. Cocks, whom he brought from Doncaster. The locomotive drawing office staff was below strength because of the lapse of time since the last new design, and their difficulties were increased because of Bulleid's sudden changes of mind. It was not unusual for him to descend on Eastleigh at night, while the first engine was under construction, tell the night foreman to do something, and then telephone the following morning to cancel or change the instruction. As a result some parts were finished without drawings, leaving the draughtsmen to prepare them subsequently. Consequently, component weights were not calculated carefully on the drawing board and the prototype locomotive was 5 tons heavier than the diagram weights approved by the Civil Engineer. Holes had to be cut in the frames to reduce the weight to the acceptable figure.[7]

The upper portion of the new Pacific was covered by a light plate casing. Bulleid did not believe in streamlining and his casing was not intended to have this effect. He described it as 'air-smoothing', and the shape of the engine and tender was meant to merge with that of his own flush-sided carriages. The casing also dispensed with the need for the wheel splashers, running boards and boiler lagging plates used on the conventional superstructure, so these were discarded. Bulleid had not liked the round-top firebox since the first boiler had been fitted to a Great Northern 'K2' class 2-6-0; for during the pressure test there had been a slight bulging, and transverse boiler stays had to be installed. He therefore chose a Belpaire firebox, and the top of this dictated in part the shape of the casing. The smokebox in turn followed this shape, whilst the lower part conformed to the set of the main steam pipes inside it. The casing plates were carried on channel section ribs attached to the main frames. As the modified Lemaître blastpipe was being used, the chimney was of large diameter. It was a plain stovepipe affair because its shape was hidden by the casing, and it was made of thin steel plate so that only a light plate roof to the smokebox was needed to support it.[8]

To keep the weight down, Bulleid took advantage of the advance made in electric welding to replace heavy castings as far as possible by parts made of steel plates, cut to shape and joined by welding. Similarly, weight was saved by adopting a steel all-welded firebox. (No other CME had dared at that time to make such extensive use of electric welding.) A steel firebox was, in fact, necessary, because of the high pressure and temperature that he had selected for his boiler. He was determined that it should never be short of steam; hence the huge grate area of 48sq ft and the boiler pressure of 280lb/sq in, which was higher than any other used in the British Isles except on one or two experimental locomotives. He also aimed at a superheat temperature of 400°C, as used by Chapelon on his rebuilt Pacific of 1929. For such figures copper was not considered suitable for the firebox, because of likely trouble in maintenance. Two thermic syphons were fitted in the firebox, connecting the lower part of the tubeplate to the crown. Their syphonic action added to the water circulation of the boiler and increased the heating surface at the most effective part, that is, within the firebox and above the firebed.[9] To accommodate them, the brick arch was in three sections — a centre section between the syphons, and outer sections between the syphons and the firebox sides. The thermic syphons conferred an additional benefit, in that they gave extra rigidity to the firebox and supported the crown sheet; thus affording a safeguard, additional to that provided by six fusible plugs, against a collapse of the crown sheet. Indeed, the syphons saved at least one disaster when all six fusible plugs went and the thermic syphons kept the firebox crown up.[10]

Bulleid chose a diameter of 6ft 2in for the coupled wheels to assist in obtaining a high tractive effort. This probably reflected his experience with Gresley's 'P2' class 2-8-2 express locomotives and 'V2' 2-6-2 mixed traffic locomotives which showed that wheels of this size were no bar to high speeds. (Maunsell, before him, had built one of his Nelsons' with 6ft 3in wheels, which did not detract from its fast running.) In addition, the reduction in diameter from the more normal 6ft 7in of a Southern express engine helped to keep within the restricted height of 13ft 1in permitted by the SR composite loading gauge. Because Bulleid did not want a higher piston speed than 2,000ft/sec, he decided on a cylinder stroke of 24in.[11] He chose three cylinders and this, as we

Below: 'Merchant Navy' No 21C1 as built in 1941. The weights quoted refer to Nos 21C3-10.

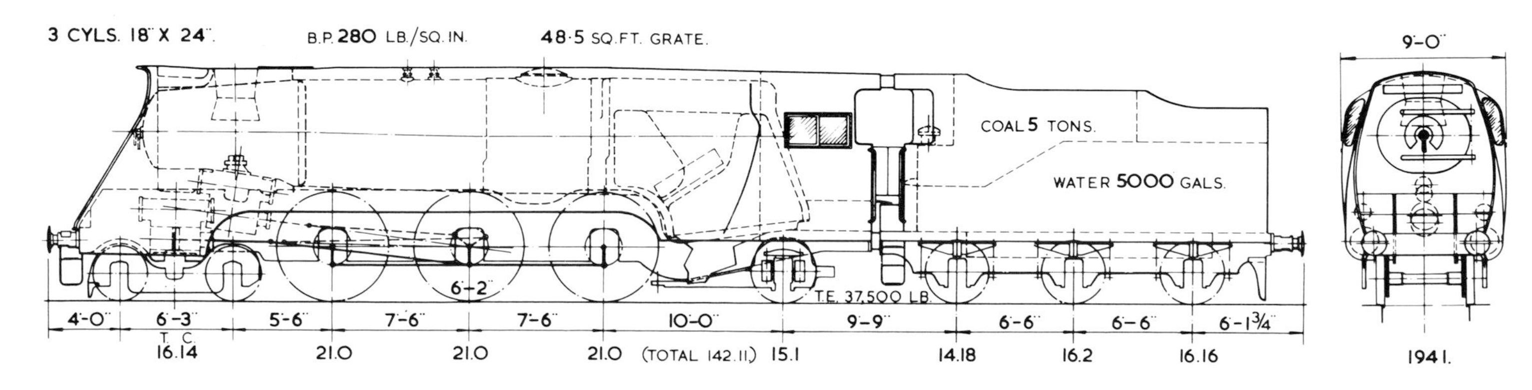

have seen, enabled him to omit reciprocating balance. Three cylinders of 24in stroke entailed a cylinder diameter of 18in to get the tractive effort he wanted. The outside cylinders were slightly inclined at 1 in 40, whilst the inside cylinder's inclination was steeper at 1 in 7¾. To permit the passages from the valves to the cylinders to be as straight as possible, outside admission valves were employed, instead of the inside admission customary with piston valves. This also freed the rocker shaft bushes from high-pressure steam. The exhaust passages from the outside cylinders were connected to the inside exhaust passage by large section pipes. Over the inside exhaust cavity was mounted the modified Lemaître blastpipe with its five jets, each of 2 ⅝in dia.[12]

Bulleid decided to make a complete departure from standard practice by enclosing the motion in an oil bath between the frames. This was intended to eradicate weaknesses in the traditional methods of lubrication, which high speeds and long non-stop runs on the LMS and LNER had revealed, and to eliminate the wear in motion details caused by grit. It would also reduce the large number of oiling points, of which some on the inside motion were awkwardly placed, that the driver had to attend to in preparing a locomotive — and at least one modern express engine had over 90.[13] This latter advantage, however, was somewhat modified by the loss of the driver's visual inspection as he went round with his oil can. The belief too, that grit causes much wear in the motion is erroneous, because grit cannot work its way in where oil is working out. It has never been found necessary to fit seals to keep dirt out.[14]

It would not have been practicable to fit three sets of normal Walschaerts valve gear within the limited confines of the oil bath, so Bulleid designed an ingenious miniaturised version. The outside return cranks and inside eccentric of the conventional Walschaerts layout for three cylinders were replaced by a three-throw crankshaft, driven by two inverted-tooth chains, which actuated the expansion links. One chain was horizontal, running from the crank axle to an intermediate sprocket wheel, and allowing for a rise and fall of the crank axle on its springs. From this sprocket the second chain connected downwards to the three-throw crankshaft. The intermediate sprocket cradle was adjustable so that chain tension could be corrected during repairs. Each valve was driven by an arm and link between the valve heads, where there was room for them in the exhaust cavity. The valve heads were not connected by spindles.

The valve gear was arranged as for inside admission, and to cater for outside admission the movement of the arms was reversed by a rocker shaft. All three rockers were connected by a shaft passing transversely through the three cylinders. To enable the three sets of valve gear to fit into the space between the frames, the full throw of the expansion links was made less than that required to give full travel to the valves, and this was made good by making the rocker arms of unequal length in the proportion of 3 to 8, so that 1½in of movement in the radius rod gave 4in of travel to the valve. The inside connecting rod, crank axle, big end, little end, inside crosshead and slide bars, and the three sets of valve motion were all contained in the oil bath. Two gear pumps driven by a chain off the three-throw crankshaft delivered oil over these parts by means of perforated pipes. It was all highly ingenious thinking by Bulleid.[15]

In order to remove the trouble of cracked spokes and the tendency of spoked wheel centres to distort, Bulleid, in conjunction with the Sheffield firm of Firth Brown, designed a type of wheel centre for the coupled wheels which was very similar to the American 'Boxpok' pattern. It was called the BFB (Bulleid-Firth-Brown) and was stronger and 10% lighter than a spoked wheel. The bogie was of the same type as the satisfactory 'Lord Nelson' pattern, though shorter, whilst the pony truck was a new Delta type with a three-point suspension to improve the riding of the engine. Bulleid had designed the springing of his locomotive to give as comfortable a ride as possible.

For front-end lubrication there were three mechanical lubricators, one for each cylinder, placed in an enclosure below the smokebox door, so that the lubricator ratchets could be driven off the valve rocker shafts.

The steam reversing gear was an inexplicable choice, because Bulleid had asked various people what kind of reverser they would like on the new engines, and all had replied that they wanted the same screw type as fitted to the 'Nelsons' and 'Schools'.[16]

The cab was well laid out and gave a better standard of comfort and protection for the engine crew than almost any other British locomotive then running. The fittings in frequent use by the driver were on the left, or driving, side and those used by the fireman were on the right. Both injectors were on the fireman's side, to save him crossing the footplate, and both were straight injectors; for Bulleid had recognised that exhaust injectors were finicky, only repairable in works, and the fuel saving claimed for them very questionable. Electric lighting was installed, with headlamps at front and rear, lights under the casing over the wheels, lights in the cab, and independent light fittings for the reverser, water gauges, and injectors; all supplied from a small steam-driven generator. The firedoors were steam-operated, for the first time in British practice, and were opened by the fireman pressing a foot pedal.[17]

Bulleid's final major innovation was a symbolic numbering for his locomotives which was derived from Continental practice. The number of coupled axles was denoted by a letter, which in this case was C for 3. The letter was preceded by figures for the number of carrying axles before and after the coupled wheels respectively; eg 21 represented a leading bogie and a trailing pony truck. After the letter came the serial number of the locomotive; thus, the first Pacific was 21C1. Unfortunately Bulleid never consulted the Running Department, who would have to use this system, and they heartily disliked it.[18]

The engines were given the names of shipping companies which used the Southern Railway's ports (though the first was named *Channel Packet* after the Southern's own ships), and they were collectively known as the 'Merchant Navy' class. The name of the shipping line appeared on a roundel, in the centre of which was its house flag, and on one side of the roundel was 'Merchant' and on the other side 'Navy Class'.

On the outbreak of war in 1939 all express trains were suspended, so it was singularly untimely that when on 10 March 1941 No 21C1 was named *Channel Packet* by the Minister of Transport at Eastleigh Works, the publicity hand-out described it as an express locomotive. The Works staff, who were now engaged in the production of military equipment and who had been bombed in the process, naturally thought that any engines they were building should be in furtherance of the war effort. They accordingly protested to Bulleid, who promptly has 'mixed traffic' substituted for 'express'.[19]

No 21C2 was named *Union Castle* in June 1941, and after the ceremony the engine hauled a special train taking the Union Castle Line Directors to Merstham for lunch. The engine failed near Norwood on the return journey and the guests were taken rather ingnominiously back to Cannon Street behind an LBSCR 'I3' class 4-4-2T. This dismal debut was followed by an even more ill-starred journey. Bulleid had claimed that one of his 'Merchant Navy' class could take a 20-coach train from Waterloo to Exeter and back, and he asked for a trial to demonstrate this. The trial was arranged for Sunday 9 November 1941, and S. C. Townroe rode in the train, which carried the Assistant General Manager of the SR, representatives of other railways' CMEs, and members of the technical press. The engine was No 21C3 *Royal Mail*, and the first scheduled stop, for water only, was Salisbury. There No 21C2 *Union Castle* was prudently kept ready as a stand-by. The 20-coach train made an impressive sight leaving Waterloo and it ran well until it slowed down at Farnborough and came to a dead stand at Basingstoke with a broken rocker shaft. An 'H15' mixed traffic 4-6-0 was put on to haul the train to Salisbury where it was replaced by *Union Castle*. Affairs did not improve, for *Union Castle* was unable to maintain the full brake vacuum, and Exeter was reached three hours late. In order to get the unfortunate guests back to London in reasonable time, the length of the train was reduced to eight coaches, into which they were crammed, and a 'King Arthur' was produced for the return journey. It was bad luck that the 'Arthur' added to the afflictions of the day by running short of steam! The press remained charitably silent about this unhappy day, but Sir Eustace Missenden, the General Manager, requested Bulleid to keep his Pacifics west of Salisbury until the Locomotive Testing Staff had got them to work more reliably. This ban lasted for some time.[20]

The troubles that plagued these engines (and also those who operated and maintained them) and the reasons for them are discussed in the following chapter.

Notes

1 Bulleid, H. A. V.; information to the Author
2 Townroe, S. C.,; information to the Author
3 Harrison, J. F.; information to the Author
4 *ibid*
5 Townroe, *op cit*
6 Bulleid, H. A. V.; *Master Builders of Steam*; London, Ian Allan Ltd, 1963, p88
7 Townroe, *op cit*
8 Bulleid, H. A. V.; *Master Builders of Steam*, pp76-7, 90. Allen, C. J. and Townroe, S. C.; *The Bulleid Pacifics of the Southern*; London, Ian Allan Ltd, 1951, p12
9 Bulleid; *Master Builders of Steam*, p91
10 Allen & Townroe; *op cit*, p13
11 Allen, C. J.; *British Pacific Locomotives*; London, Ian Allan Ltd, 1962, pp159 and 163
12 Allen & Townroe, *op cit* p14
13 *ibid*
14 Townroe, information to the Author
15 Allen & Townroe, *op cit*, p14
16 Townroe, information to the Author
17 Allen & Townroe, *op cit*, p16
18 Townroe, information to the Author
19 *ibid*
20 *ibid*

Below: No 21C1 *Channel Packet* the first of the new generation of Bulleid Pacifics, seen here in as built condition in 1941. *BR*

Top left: The front of *Channel Packet* in as built condition. Large cast metal ownership and number plates, including 'unlucky' Southern horseshoe. Air intake above smokebox door leading to the chimney. Photograph dated March 1941. *BR*

Top right: A head on view of No 21C12 *United States Lines* clearly showing the smokebox circlet, complete with building date. The electric headcode lamps can also be seen. On the Southern the headcode showed the route that the train was to take, on the other companies the headcode showed the class of train. *Crown Copyright, National Railway Museum*

Above: *Channel Packet,* with the modified version of the air-smoothed casing around the smokebox, as running in June 1949. *P. Ransome Wallis*

Right: No 21C4 *Cunard White Star* stands at Waterloo heading a boat train special to Southampton for the maiden voyage of RMS *Queen Elizabeth* as a passenger liner on 16 October 1946. *Topical Press Agency*

R.M.S.
QUEEN
ELIZABETH
21C4

Above: No 21C13 *Blue Funnel* attracts admirers at Waterloo, prior to departing with the 'Bournemouth Belle'. *F. G. Reynolds*

Left: The front of *Royal Mail* in 1941, note horseshoe modified to circlet and the enlarged air space above the smokebox. Compare with that of *Channel Packet*. *BR*

Above right: No 21C3 *Royal Mail* photographed in shop grey livery in 1941. *BR*

Centre right: No 21C5 *Canadian Pacific* this was one of the batch of locomotives that entered service with asbestos casing. The horizontal ridge acted as a strengthener. *Modern Transport Collection*

Bottom right: No 21C12 *United States Lines* photographed in shop grey livery in 1945. Note revisions to air-smoothed casing — inverted trough above smokebox and deflectors. *BR*

SOUTHERN
ROYAL MAIL
MERCHANT NAVY CLASS
21C3
21C 3
SOUTHERN

SOUTHERN
21C 5
CANADIAN PACIFIC
MERCHANT NAVY CLASS
SOUTHERN
21C 5

SOUTHERN
21C 12
UNITED STATES LINES
MERCHANT NAVY CLASS
21C 12

Left: ***Canadian Pacific,*** **prior to running a special.**
Topical Press Agency

Below: No 21C4 ***Cunard White Star*** **heads the down 'Bournemouth Belle' near Vauxhall, circa 1946.** *IAL*

Right: No 21C6 ***Peninsular & Oriental SN Co*** **sports the first of several modifications to the front end, in an effort to reduce the smoke clinging effect. Seen near Worting junction.** *IAL*

Far right: The driver leans out of his cab in an endeavour to obtain a better view.
S. C. Townroe

Below right: The Southern's prestige boat train, the 'Golden Arrow', soon after reintroduction in 1946 with ***Channel Packet*** **at its head sporting headboard and arrows.** *IAL*

21C 6

GOLDEN
ARROW
21C 1

SOUTHERN
21C14

Left: No 21C14 *Nederland Line* with the 10.41 up Bournemouth train.
C. Cunningham

Above: No 21C2 sports the original front end arrangement while No 21C8 *Orient Line* carries the final design to improve smoke lifting.
Modern Transport Collection/IAL

Below: The driver of No 21C17 *Belgium Marine* looks back for the guard's signal at Brockenhurst with a down Waterloo-Bournemouth express.
P. R. Turne

Above: No 21C4 awaits the arrival of the 'non-stop' 'Devon Belle' at Wilton South to change engines, note the nameboard on the smoke deflectors. *IAL*

Above right: Southampton Central, No 21C18 *British India Line* with the first postwar 'Bournemouth Belle' on 7 October 1946. *F. F. Moss*

Right: No 21C7 *Aberdeen Commonwealth* heads a lengthy train of empty milk tankers returning to the West Country, near West Weybridge in August 1947. *Wethersett Collection/IAL*

SOUTHERN
35
THE
BOURNEMOUTH
BELLE
21C18
SOUTHERN
139
21C 7

4
The 'Merchant Navy' troubles

As a result of Missenden's instruction, the 10 Pacifics of the original order were sent to Salisbury mpd and in that place also the members of the Testing Staff assembled. Salisbury, fortunately, was a very convenient testing headquarters because it was a comparatively short distance from Eastleigh, with a direct rail connection. Spare parts could thus be readily supplied and crippled locomotives could be despatched easily to the works for attention.

Soon after tests began a curious fault pattern emerged. Changes in power output occurred without obvious reason. This, it was afterwards discovered, could be corrected by putting the reversing lever nearer towards full travel and opening the regulator. The cause of these changes was eventually traced to the steam-operated reversing gear, which habitually crept away from the position in which it had been set. It was not possible to rectify this entirely, although the gear was modified considerably to make it less erratic and thus enable the driver to make smaller adjustments to the cut-off.[1]

This was by no means the only trouble encountered and signalmen at junction stations became accustomed to being informed at short notice that one of the 'Packets' (as they became known) would have to quit its train at their station. One of the most frequent causes of failure was a broken rocker shaft, which was indicated by the engine losing two beats. The enclosure of the motion made it difficult for the driver to detect impending failure by stopping for examination. The primary cause of broken rockers was traced to an unbalanced steam chest pressure, that is a pressure difference between the two ends of the piston valves. The immediate solution was to strengthen the rocker shafts by making them 4in in diameter instead of $2\frac{1}{2}$in, and Bulleid ordered 50 spare rocker shafts to be made and sent to Salisbury. Later the steam chests were re-designed to include a balancing cavity.[2]

The Testing Staff evolved a quick method of checking trouble. A suspected engine would be shunted into a siding and the rails oiled. With the brake on, the regulator was then opened. If nothing was heard amiss the engine would be returned to traffic, and, as likely as not, would work normally again. One day, for instance, an engine was taken off a train at Yeovil because it was behaving sluggishly. A siding was oiled and the wheels spun, but nothing wrong could be detected. It was accordingly put back into service on another train and behaved satisfactorily. Such erratic conduct was inherent in the valve gear and was caused by backlash in the many joints, amplified by the 3:8 unequal arms of the rocker shafts.[3] The chains proved unsuitable for operating valve gear with any degree of precision. There was no stretching of the links themselves, but in course of time the wear of pins and holes, and also of the teeth of the intermediate sprocket wheel, had the same effect. At the general overhaul of some of the engines the length of the longer chain (which had 118 links) was found to have increased by as much as 6in.[4]

Higher mileage engines, in particular, suffered from erratic beats, but if they managed to keep time they were allowed to run until the opportunity occurred for a major examination. On one occasion a down Sunday boat train was stopped by signals near Dover motive power depot. When it re-started the fitter-in-charge at the mpd noticed that it had only three beats and a bull-like roar up the chimney. He thought that the driver would ask him to look at the engine when he came in to turn; and that, if so, he would tell him to dump it and take another. However, about an hour later the fitter-in-charge noticed that the driver had been in, turned, and watered, and was waiting to go out on an up train. Accordingly he went casually up to the driver and commented on the odd noises; to which the driver replied: 'She came down like it, so she can go back like it.' Later the fitter telephoned the foreman at Stewarts Lane mpd, to which the engine belonged, only to be told that the driver had booked off without any complaints! When the engine was eventually checked by fitters it was found to have one valve uncoupled, and it was ascertained that it had been in that condition for some days.[5]

The oil sump, so excellent in theory, turned out to be the most unfortunate choice. R. L. Curl, a Senior Locomotive Draughtsman, had been given the job of designing an inside connecting rod which was to be lubricated by a pipe from an oil box at the small end, by means of a self-acting plunger group. He had not solved the means of fastening the oil pipe along the connecting rod, without drilling it in any way, when the plan was dropped and the oil bath motion substituted.[6] Bulleid had got the idea from the sump of a car, but the two were not really comparable. The car sump is unstressed by frame flexure, whereas, by being fabricated as part of the main frames, Bulleid's oil bath could not remain oil tight. Again, the car crankshaft, unlike a locomotive driving axle, does not move up and down and so can be sealed against oil loss. The car engine bearings, too, are pressure-fed, whereas Bulleid relied on splash-and-spray lubrication which automobile engineers had discarded in early days. Another important difference was that condensation in a car sump is kept to negligible proportions by suitable ventilation; but in Bulleid's Pacifics the steamy conditions and large changes in temperature resulted in condensation serious enough to cause the oil to emulsify and to corrode the valve gear components, so that far more motion pins had to be replaced than with the more normal exposed Walschaerts gear. The frame flexure that caused sump joints to leak, also either broke the lengthy steam pipes between the superheater header and the cylinders, or produced leakage at their joints, shrouding the front end in steam. More flexible joints with 'concertina' sections were a palliative rather than a cure.[7]

Oil consumption was staggering. It escaped from the valve spindle guides in the front of the sump; it got on the driving wheels, causing slipping; and it was thrown up on to the boiler lagging, causing fires. Some engines caught fire so badly that the local fire brigades had to be summoned. it proved impossible to prevent oil leakage where the driving axle passed through the frames, as well as through joints in the bath structure and cracks in the metal caused by vibration and flexing of the frames on curves.[8] Better seals were provided for the driving axles, but no adequate solution was found for the other leaks.[9]

On many locomotives failure of inside big-ends was an all too common occurrence, and the damage could be so serious that detection of impending trouble was important. Routine inspection by the driver was valuable and on Gresley's Pacifics this was supplemented by a device (known as a 'stink bomb') producing a strong purfume to warn the driver that all was not well. But the enclosed motion on the Bulleid Pacifics prevented the driver from either inspecting or smelling or even hearing knocks. Failure, therefore, came unheralded and abruptly, with a protruding connecting rod which had knocked a hole in the sump, emptying bits of metal and gallons of oil on to the track. Some improvement was made to the middle big end lubrication by re-designing the oil-collecting box on the top of the big end to stop oil, already caught by the spray pipe, from being thrown out again.

The sump had other disadvantages; its enclosure of the inside crosshead precluded a cottered connection with the piston rod and entailed using a forged crosshead and piston rod; the piston itself being secured by a nut and taper fit. This latter had been a Drummond practice on the LSWR, and it had also been used on the LMS until Stanier banned it from his engines. It was known to be potentially troublesome because, sooner or later, every engine had a carry-over of water which tended to compress the piston on the rod and slightly loosen the nut. Cylinder cocks, blocked by carbon or pieces of broken rings could start a chain of events culminating in a piston and nut breaking through the cylinder cover. Bulleid used plug cocks for the cylinder drains, as did Dugald Drummond, and these were prone to stick and so buckle the cock operating rod. A Pacific once arrived at Waterloo with an outside cylinder cover missing and no piston. When this was discovered the driver admitted that he had 'heard a bump' when passing Hook, 42 miles back, but the engine was running well so he did not stop. He was aware of a lot of steam drifting around the front, but this was not unusual with the Pacifics. The missing pieces were indeed found at Hook.

The sumps, as already stated, relieved drivers of some oiling duties, but they had to be topped up daily by the fitters, who also had to drain off the water from condensation. Furthermore, on more conventional locomotives, 'blows' from pistons or valves could be checked by the time-honoured routine of 'round the wheel' inspection, which was instilled into every budding driver. Big ends, for instance, could be set in various positions to identify a suspect piston or valve. But on the Pacifics it was much more difficult to ascertain the positions of valves and valve gear, and fault finding had to be left to the fitters. Another fitters' nightmare was presented by the boiler casing, for leaks in the pipework concealed behind it were difficult to trace. Unofficial access doors were sometimes cut through the casing and carefully welded up and painted over when the job was completed.

The position of the three mechanical lubricators below the smokebox door turned out to be singularly unfortunate because they became smothered with smokebox dust and ash, which could hardly be prevented from getting into the lubricators when the lids were opened for filling with oil. In an effort to remedy this, a three-branch filler pipe was fitted so that oil could be supplied without opening the lids. The drawback to this solution was that it was not easy to see, from the drop in oil level, whether each lubricator was functioning.

Slipping by these locomotives was excessive. At certain places, particularly where an engine would start a train, the heads of the rails could become so damaged and burn-marked that they would have to be replaced because of the risk of subsequent rail fracture. Slipping also caused bent coupling rods, which had to be removed and sent to works to be straightened. Coupling rods, too, were found to be repeatedly bending and straigthening themselves till they eventually broke; consequently they had to be re-designed. Slipping was caused partly by the oil from the sump getting on the rails, but partly, also, by the soft springing on the coupled wheels. The springs became soft with use or suffered broken plates, so that some of the adhesion weight was transferred to the bogie and pony truck. On a 'West Country' class engine, for instance, the weights should have been 15ton 15cwt on the bogie, 18ton 15cwt on each coupled axle, and 14ton 5cwt on the trailing truck. In a typical case these became 16ton 5cwt on the bogie; on the three coupled axles respectively 17ton, 18ton and 18ton 5cwt; and 16ton 15cwt on the pony truck. Bulleid, as already stated, had designed this soft springing to give a comfortable ride; but eventually it had to be replaced by harder springs, as used on the British Railways Class 7 Pacifics, and this cured the trouble. Engines reported as slipping, despite careful handling, would be stopped and sent to Eastleigh Works weigh table for spring adjustment. When, later on, the stronger springs were fitted, they made the riding slightly less comfortable but reduced slipping and also the number of broken springs. These latter had been a particular nuisance, firstly because replacing a broken spring is a difficult task and secondly because broken springs could not be seen through the solid coupled wheel centres. The altered springing probably explains the conflicting opinions that have been expressed about the riding of these engines. C. J Allen described the Bulleid Pacifics as some of the smoothest riding locomotives in the country;[10] whereas O. S. Nock says that they were very steady but not always smooth riding and that they never glided like a 'Duchess'; the vibration being nearly always there.[11]

The sanding arrangements were a contributory cause of slipping. The sand boxes were under the casing, in which small sliding doors gave access to the filling hole. To fill them it was necessary to find a ladder and climb up it carrying a heavy bucket of sand. Filling the boxes was thus liable to be skimped, rendering the engine even more liable to slip through lack of sand. Furthermore, it was difficult to get all the sand into the filling hole, so that some would spill down the side of the casing on to the outside slide bars. For this reason the front sand boxes were later abandoned.[12]

The bronze driving axleboxes developed fatigue cracks after a time, which entailed re-casting in this expensive material.[13] Bulleid, however, had been used to them on the LNER,[14] and had chosen them on the grounds that they were easily made in a railway foundry and the value of the metal was never lost.[15] But this argument overlooked the cost of machining the castings.

The steam operated firedoors, though excellent in theory, were disappointing in practice. They depended for satisfactory operation upon correct adjustment of the height of the operating pedal above the floor boards and of its position, to suit the stance of each fireman, and also on the adjustment of the steam valve so that the doors opened and closed gently but not too slowly. These two adjustments were made neither easily nor quickly, and could thus interfere with the fireman's work; while if the steam valve adjustment was not exactly right, the fireman could find himself swinging a loaded shovel at closed doors, or perhaps the doors would close before he could withdraw his shovel. Most firemen, therefore, preferred to leave the doors open during a round of firing, using the hand lever to open and close them. In due course the CME Department wrote to the Locomotive Running Department asking if the steam fittings were required, because their condition, when examined in workshops, indicated that they were inoperative through disuse. The Running Department promptly replied that they did not want the steam fittings and would like them removed.

The arrangement for smoke lifting at the front end proved ineffective. It was surprising, indeed, that it was ever adopted, because it was very similar to a method tried on LNER 'A3' class Pacific No 2747 *Coronach* in 1931, and soon abandoned. In 1942 a scale wooden model of a 'Merchant Navy' was sent to Southampton University for wind tunnel tests, and after lengthy experiments a much better configuration was devised. The deflector plates, incorporated in this new design, were fixed to the boiler casing by brackets at the top edge and spot welded. This fixture gave rise to a peculiar accident. When a locomotive was working the 'Devon Belle', large metal plates bearing this name were bolted to the smoke deflectors. One day in May 1947 as the down 'Belle' was passing an up train near Axminster the offside deflector and nameplate came off — the crumpled mass of metal doing considerable damage and causing crippling injuries to one of the passengers. The passenger submitted a large claim for compensation and employed an expert witness who said that the spot-welding of the brackets was quite inadequate to withstand wind stresses from traffic on the adjacent line, and that the extra load of the nameplates had been overlooked. The plaintiff was successful. There had been a prior warning, for a deflector plate on a 'King Arthur' had been bent double, owing to a missing bolt at the bottom front corner, when meeting another train in 1943. On the Maunsell engines, however, the upper edge of the deflector plate was firmly clipped to the hand rail, and in this incident the plate did not come off. A notice was sent out at the time to all depots that deflector plates must be checked for security; but it would appear that this was not brought to the notice of the CME, though his department would have had a copy.[16]

In 1946 there were a number of cases of bent intermediate drawbars amongst the Pacifics at Nine Elms; and one of them, after working a boat train to Southampton, became derailed in the Old Docks when turning on a triangle with sharp curves, even though there were unofficial dock gauges of 4ft 9in. Subsequent tests showed that flexibility was inadequate and the intermediate drawgear had to be redesigned.

Maintenance difficulties in general were enhanced because Bulleid issued no drawings or descriptions of the dozens of novel and unfamiliar items that the running sheds were expected to maintain. A mechanical inspector was needed who could help both drivers and fitting staff, and who could advise Bulleid as to the difficulties and failures. Bulleid's senior outdoor inspector did indeed report to him about the early failures, but it is a measure of Bulleid's weakness in communications with his staff that he received that information coldly and blamed bad workmanship. As a result the incensed inspector refused to see him again. Townroe had heard of these allegations of bad workmanship, but, as far as he knew, Bulleid never substantiated such charges with the Locomotive Running Superintendent. As CME he had, of course, the right, and indeed the responsibility, of following up any instances of bad workmanship, whether caused by the workshops or shed staff.[17] During the building of the 'Merchant Navy' class Bulleid made numerous changes, with the result that the Fitting and Machine Shops were littered with half-finished castings and forgings consigned to the scrap bin.[18]

One minor, but not unimportant, example of the maintenance difficulties caused by lack of information is provided by the Klinger pattern of water gauge which had never been seen before on the Southern Railway. It consisted basically of a thick strip of glass clamped in a cast steel frame and having prismatic grooves on its water side. The advantages claimed were that there was no danger of its bursting or blowing out, and that the water level was visible very clearly. However there were repeated failures of joints which were just as bad as burst glasses in gauges of the conventional kind. The Locomotive Running Department requested advice from the Klinger staff. It transpired that dealing with these failures, as well as the routine renewal of the glasses, involved taking the gauges to a bench, preparing the joint faces with care, and re-assembling — a new technique and one which entailed additional work by the fitters. On the Southern Railway drivers had previously been responsible for gauge glasses; spares being kept in every engine tool box.[19]

The extra maintenance needed by the Pacifics was recognised by increasing the number of fitters. In a large running shed, before the advent of the Pacifics, there was one fitter for every six engines; but when the Pacifics arrived the establishment was increased to two fitters for every six engines.

Apart from the engine itself, certain troubles were experienced with the early tenders. The tank sides were weak and they frequently developed splits, of which there was visible evidence in long runs of welding. Improvement was effected by strengthening the tender structure with internal stays and adding baffles to reduce the surge of water. Another weakness in the tender lay in the water connection to the two injectors. The water was taken from a small well in the tender bottom, containing a sieve which was accessible from inside the tank. This sieve was easily blocked by small coal which found its way into the tenders, cutting off water to both injectors and causing the engine to become a total failure. Separate feeds and strainers were accordingly fitted when the tenders were rebuilt.

It is pleasant to change from these criticisms to the design of the boiler; for Bulleid's boiler was probably as good as any that has ever been produced for a locomotive anywhere in the world. Its output was astounding and its insensibility to the quality of the coal was of inestimable benefit in the postwar

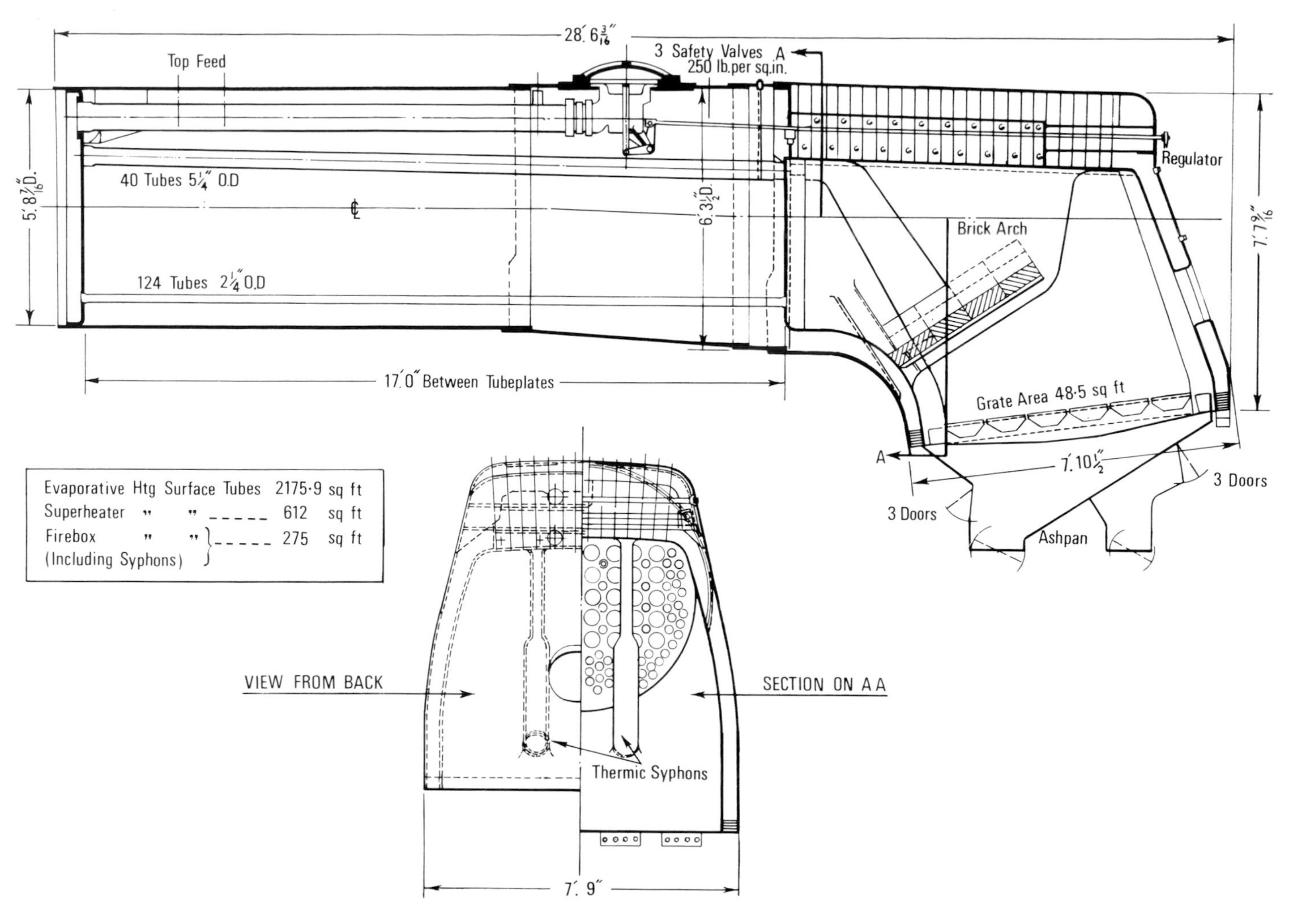

Above: Sectional side and end elevations of the boiler as fitted to the last 20 'Merchant Navy' engines and the five spares. But showing the reduced boiler pressure which was altered from 1952 onwards.

years. There was occasional cracking in the fire zone between stays of the steel firebox, but this could be rectified easily by welding. The French TIA (*Traitement Intégral Armand*) water treatment was adopted and this allowed boilers to undergo 28 days between washouts, as compared with the normal 7-10 days. The equipment for controlling the correct dosage was rather elaborate, but in due course this was replaced by a simpler system.

The last of the first 10 'Merchant Navy' Pacifics was completed in August 1942. It was over two years before construction began on another 10, and these embodied various modifications which had been incorporated in their predecessors. The first of the second batch entered traffic in December 1944 and the last in June 1945. The boilers differed from those of the first 10 in that they had the top and bottom of the front ring parallel, whilst the bottom of the rear ring was tapered — the reverse of the tapering arrangement in the earlier boilers. The intention was to save weight and to lower the water capacity of the boiler without altering the steam generating capacity or the heating surface. In course of time boilers of either pattern could appear on any engine. A third batch of 10 engines was ordered just before Nationalisation, and these were completed between September 1948 and April 1949.

Notes

1 Townroe, S. C.; information to the Author
Allen, C. J.; *British Pacific Locomotives;* London, Ian Allan Ltd, 1962, pp159-163
2 Townroe, *op cit*
3 *ibid*
4 Allen, *op cit*, pp165-7
5 Ing, A.; information
6 Curl, R. L.; information
7 Townroe, *op cit*
8 Allen, *op cit*
9 Townroe, *op cit*
10 Allen, *op cit*, pp159-163
11 Nock, O. S.; *Southern Steam;* Newton Abbot, David & Charles, 1966, pp152-160
12 Townroe, *op cit*
13 *ibid*
14 Hodgson, J. T. and Lake, C. S.; *Locomotive Management;* London, Tothill Press, 1954, Tenth Edn, pp126, 129
15 Bulleid, H. A. V.; *Master Builders of Steam;* London, Ian Allan Ltd, 1963, p90
16 Townroe, *op cit*
17 *ibid*
18 Curl, *op cit*
19 Hodgson and Lake, *op cit*, pp97-100
Townroe, *op cit*

Above: No 35016 *Elders Fyffes* on an up West of England–Waterloo express at Whimple in July 1955. *T. Lewis*

Left: No 35028 *Clan Line* heading the 09.30 Victoria–Dover express through the cutting south of Knockholt in March 1951. *E. D. Bruton*

Below left: No 35009 *Shaw Savill* sets out from Waterloo with a down train. *Brian Morrison*

Above right: No 35020 *Bibby Line* on the down 'Bournemouth Belle' near Shawford in August 1952. *J. Davenport*

Right: No 35014 *Nederland Line* on the up 'Belle' and taking water at Southampton Central with No 30850 *Lord Nelson* alongside. *IAL*

35020
35020
THE
BOURNEMOUTH
BELLE

THE
BOURNEMOUTH
BELLE

THE
BOURNEMOUTH
BELLE

SOUTHERN
475
THE
DEVON BELLE

Above left: The 'Belle' headed by No 35011 *General Steam Navigation* passing Micheldever. *F. R. Hebron*

Left: The 'Devon Belle' seen between Sidmouth Junction and Whimple on 20 September 1948 headed by 'Merchant Navy' No 21C8 *Orient Line*. *P. C. Short*

Above: No 35023 *Holland-Afrika Line* with 'Atlantic Coast Express' nameboard and duty number on the route discs.
Locomotive Publishing Co/IAL

Right: The 'Golden Arrow' headed by No 35027 *Port Line* departs from Victoria at 10.00 on 3 April 1950. *D. Canning*

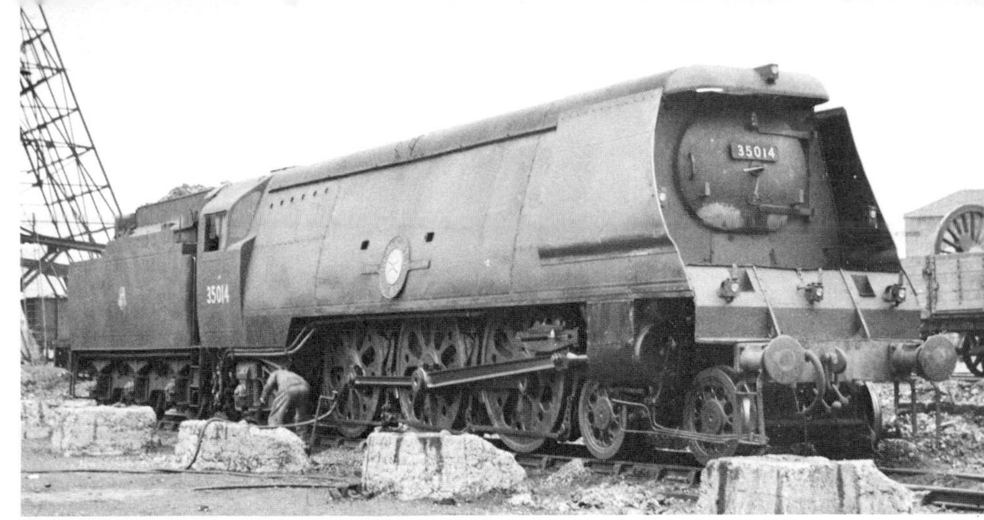

Above right: No 35014 ***Nederland Line*** **stands at Nine Elms complete with self-weighing tender.** *Brian Morrison*

Right: ***Nederland Line*** **again — this time just after Nationalisation, in SR malachite green, with no evidence of ownership displayed on the tender.** *J. H. Aston*

Below: No 35002 ***Union Castle*** **stands at Nine Elms shed on 27 March 1952. The locomotive is in the new green livery unlike the tender which is still carrying the short-lived blue livery.** *C. G. Geard*

Far right, top: No 35006 ***Peninsular & Oriental SN Co*** **leaving Yeovil Junction with an express for London, 5 June 1959.** *A. J. Coiley*

Far right, bottom: No 35005 ***Canadian Pacific*** **hauling a West of England test train with LMR carriages.** *IAL*

35006
483

35005

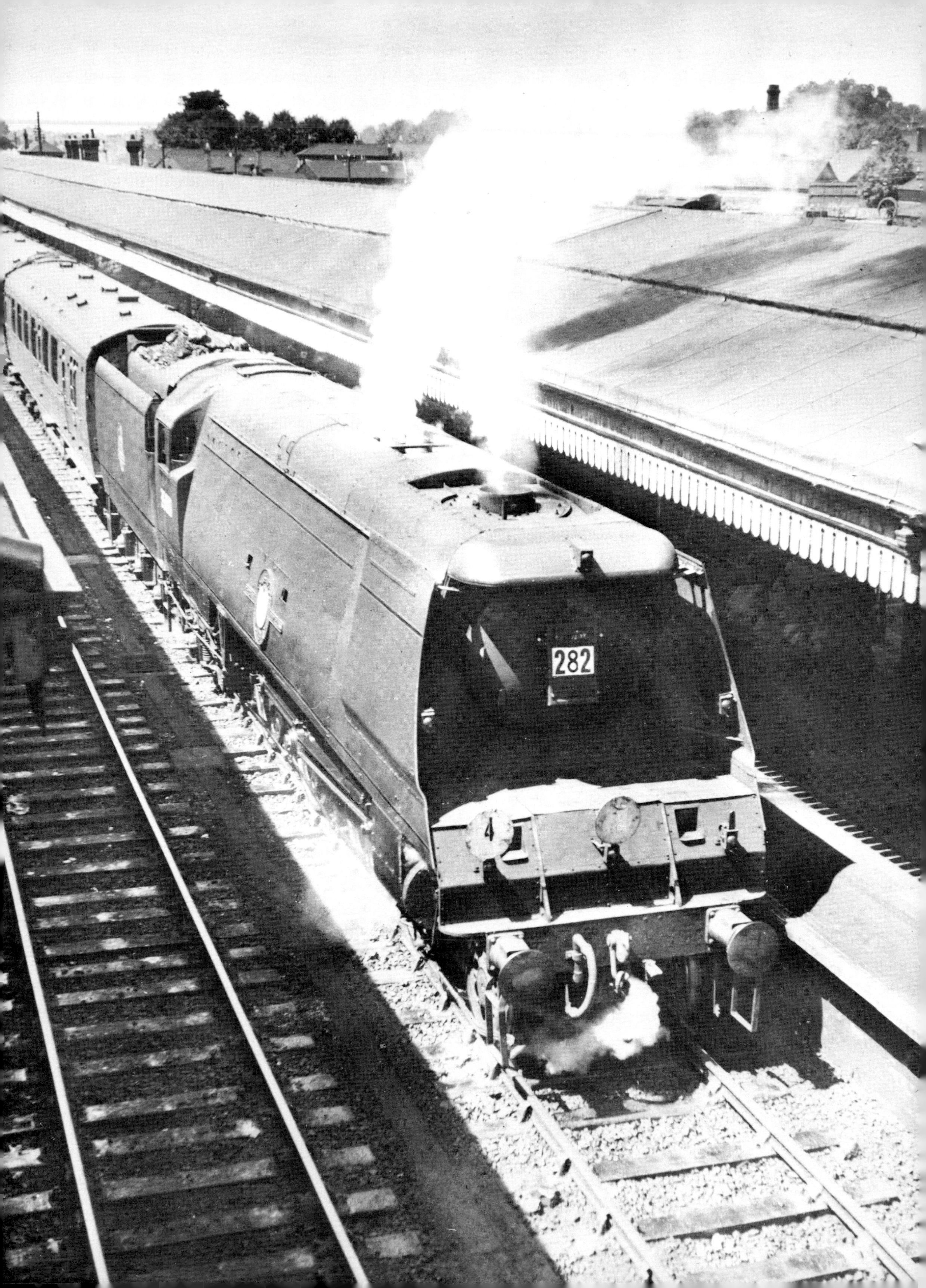
282
4

Above: No 35016 *Elders Fyffes* passing Wimbledon flyover with a down West of England express on 25 July 1953.
R. H. Turnstall

Left: Blue painted No 35024 *East Asiatic Company* stands at Exeter Central.
W. J. Reynolds

Below left: No 35022 *Holland America Line* enters Honiton tunnel with the up 'Atlantic Coast Express' minus nameboard.
F. R. Hebron/Rail Archive Stephenson

Far left: No 35019 *French Line C. G. T.* steams into Salisbury station. This was the locomotive that was fitted with a single blastpipe chimney, as clearly shown in this photograph. *G. F. Heiron*

Above: No 35028 *Clan Line* leaving Southampton Central with a down Bournemouth express on 10 September 1949. The nameplates are boarded over prior to the naming ceremony which finally took place in January 1951. *P. C. Short*

Left: No 35025 *Brocklebank Line* in early BR days, climbing the 1 in 60 gradient near Parkstone, Dorset on 10 June 1949, with an up Weymouth train. *H. Weston*

Below left: No 35028 in June 1949 at Clapham Junction with a down Bournemouth express. *C. C. E. Herbert*

Above right: No 35029 *Ellerman Lines* unusually seen at Brighton on 31 October 1955 awaiting its visit to the works. *W. M. J. Jackson*

Right: No 35026 *Lamport & Holt Line* leaves Shakespeare Cliff tunnel on the down 'Golden Arrow' on 3 November 1951. *M. E. Ware*

35029
35029
ELLERMAN
LINES

5

'Merchant Navies' and 'West Countries' in Use and on Test

The 'Merchant Navy' class had been intended to meet all the requirements of express passenger traffic on the Southern Railway's principal main lines. There were, however, a number of secondary routes which were, or could be, used for through trains of main line stock which had to be worked by the locomotives having the lesser axle loads of not more than 18tons 10cwt imposed by these routes. All the lines west of Exeter came into this secondary category, and over them ran long distance trains from Waterloo to the West Country, such as the 'Atlantic Coast Express'; but these were shortened at Exeter, or, in the summer months, subdivided into portions for Plymouth, Ilfracombe, Padstow, and Bude. The most powerful passenger or mixed traffic engines permitted west of Exeter were the Maunsell 'U' and 'N' class Moguls. These admirable engines could deal adequately with the lighter trains which formed the major part of the traffic in this area; but in more recent times it became customary to route heavy excursion and other main line specials to West Country destinations, and these often taxed the capacity of the Moguls, and could not be accelerated.

In April 1941 Brighton Drawing Office was given the task of designing 20 passenger locomotives for the West Country. In December 1942 drawings were produced for a three-cylinder 2-6-0 rather similar to the LNER 'K4' class, though with independent sets of Walschaerts valve gear, a Belpaire firebox and BFB wheels. Bulleid was apparently not happy with this solution, because the quality of the coal was deteriorating and a wide firebox seemed desirable. In 1943, therefore, the design was expanded into a 2-6-2 to accommodate such a firebox. Two factors led to the adoption of a smaller version of a 'Merchant Navy' Pacific. These were that a leading bogie would be better suited to the many curves on the routes and that, owing to wartime production difficulties, it was desirable to include as many 'Merchant Navy' features as possible. The number of engines was increased to 30, and these were ordered from Brighton Works.[1]

The aim in the design was to have the greatest power possible within a total engine weight of 86 tons and without exceeding 19 tons axle weight. Bulleid decided to retain unaltered the 'Merchant Navy' bogie, coupled wheels, axleboxes, and motion details; but to scale down the cylinders, boiler and firebox, and to reduce disposal time by improving the grate and ashpan. He also reckoned to save weight by the further application of welding.[2] The three cylinders were each 16⅜in by 24in, and the grate area was 38.25sq ft. Rocking grates were incorporated to break up clinker, and one section could be dropped to ease cleaning. There were no dampers.[3]

The first of the 'Lightweights', as they were popularly known, was completed in May 1945, and from then on they were turned out almost continuously until in January 1951 they reached the astounding total of 110 engines. In appearance they looked so like their bigger sisters that it took something of an expert to tell them apart. In order to fit on to 60ft turntables, they were slightly shorter, and the first 70 had a cab 6in narrower for the restricted loading gauge of the Mountfield tunnel on the Hastings line. Their route availability was such that they could go almost anywhere on the Southern system, except for a few branch lines. The first 48 engines and 18 of the later ones were given the names of places in the West Country and were designated the 'West Country' class. Nearly all the remainder were given names associated with the air battle of Britain in 1940 and were called the 'Battle of Britain' class — presumably a publicity decision and a pretty poor one because identical engines were separated into two classes. In practice the term 'West Country' was commonly and officially applied to all of them; but it would have been far better to have followed the Great Western Railway whose 'Star' class, for instance, included 'Queens', 'Princes', 'Abbeys' and others.

The whistles of the 'West Countries' were horizontal, mounted on the right hand side of the casing, and operated

Below: 'West Country' No 21C101 as built in 1945.

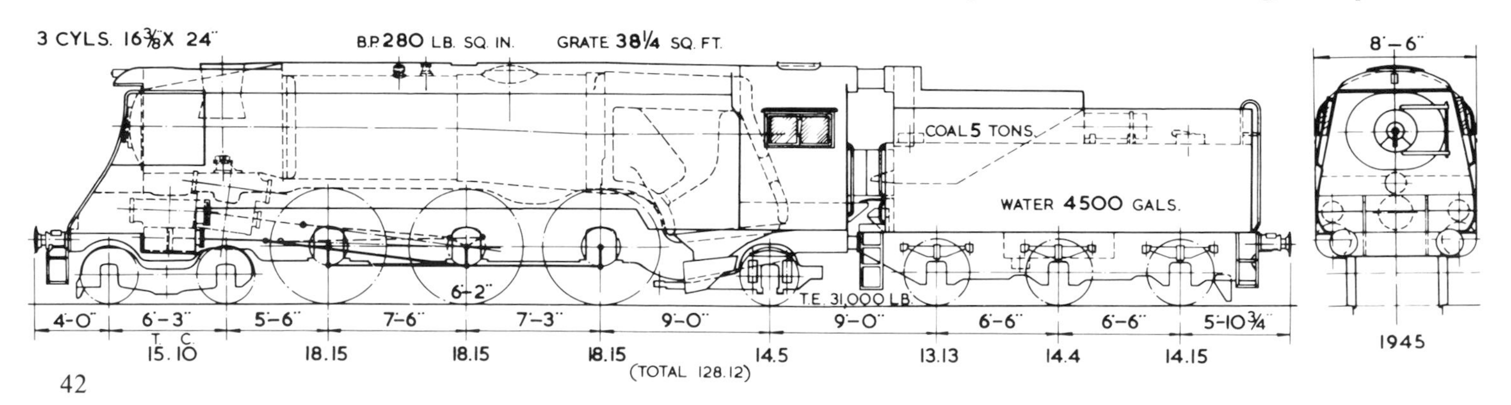

by a wire. When an engine was low in steam there was a tendency for the whistle valve to become unseated and emit a continuous low drone. Rather oddly, this was audible over a mile away but was not so easily heard close to the engine. At Exmouth Junction, where there was a number of 'West Countries', the midnight moanings began to disturb some of the citizens of Exeter and complaints were made to the police. The only way to stop the noise was to get a long ladder, open the cover, and close the whistle valve by hand. The answer to the trouble was found in substituting a rod for the wire, whereby the whistle was less liable to misbehave and could be closed down from the footplate if it did so. Many photographs of 'West Countries' show the whistle covers missing, for they often blew off and were lost, or the hinges rusted.[4]

Bulleid's improvements to grate and ashpan did not fulfill his expectations. The drop and rocking grates often stuck in the open position, so the enginemen stopped using them and fires had to be cleared laboriously through the firehole door. The absence of dampers, too, was not appreciated. H. A. V. Bulleid relates that his father asked a fireman at Waterloo what he thought of the 'West Country' class. The fireman (who presumably did not recognise the CME) was trying to avoid his engine blowing off and replied: 'You'd have thought the bloody fool who designed them would have had the sense to fit dampers.' Bulleid retorted: 'Dampers! I do not fit my engines with devices to prevent steaming.'[5] Official opinion on these matters is contained in the following memorandum of 25 July 1960, headed 'Drop Grates and Firebars — Unmodified "West Country" class Locomotives':[6]

'The grates on the above locomotives are made up of rocking bars, but there is a central frame containing a drop portion which itself contains rocking bars. Great difficulty has always been experienced in the use of the drop grate which is apt to collapse and cause a casualty. For this reason the drop grates are seldom disturbed . . . but the bearing bars sag and this causes the drop grate frames to distort, burn and collapse. Altogether this grate had been most unsatisfactory.

'All except the last 20 "West Country" class locomotives had ashpans which were open at the sides and were in fact without any form of damper. This feature had given rise to much waste of coal when the locomotive is standing, due to the lack of any means of regulating the air supply. It has also caused fires on the locomotives due to flames emerging under conditions of light blow back. The last 20 locomotives were fitted with a very complicated design of ashpan which was much complained of by the Works inasmuch as it was necessary to remove the boiler from the frames in order to carry out ashpan repairs. It was therefore agreed some years ago that as these locomotives passed through the Works the grates and ashpans as fitted to the modified locomotives would be applied to them.'

Apart from these troubles, the 'West Countries' inherited all those that went with the oil bath, the Bulleid motion, the boiler casing, the springing etc; yet there is no doubt that both classes were brilliant performers when in good condition, though at a heavy cost in maintenance and in coal, oil, and water consumption. Many drivers were lavish in their praise, but there were understandable reasons for this. When the Bulleid Pacifics made their appearance, they were so much more powerful than any other Southern passenger locomotives that drivers were bound to welcome them. Salisbury and Exmouth Junction drivers, for instance, had for years handled trains over one of the hardest stretches of main line in the country with nothing better than 'King Arthurs', and west of Exeter the N class 2-6-0s were completely outclassed by the 'West Countries'. Indeed SR drivers at Exmouth Junction and Plymouth, who worked over both the GWR and SR routes, were jubilant at getting locomotives more modern than those of their Great Western neighbours, after the feeling of inferiority they had had with their comparatively second-rate Moguls. When stopping at Exeter's St Davids station at night alongside a Great Western 'King' or 'Castle', the 'West Country' driver would turn on all his electric lighting by way of showing off his really up-to-date engine.[7]

Both classes of Pacific had a tremendous reserve of boiler capacity which enabled them to recover from signal checks in the dense traffic areas of the Eastern Section and to cope with the difficulty of its gradients, the majority of which could not be approached at high speed.

Having plenty of steam, even with a young and inexperienced fireman, the driver did not need to look anxiously at the boiler pressure gauge; nor was the cut-off setting critical, so that the vagaries of the steam reverser were of no major importance. With worn valve gear the cut-off setting could in fact read anything between 50% and full gear; though heavy spark throwing at the chimney top could warn the driver to ease the lever back a bit. The only time that the driver had to be gentle with the regulator was in coping with slipping. This could occur not only in starting but also at speed, when there would be a sudden shuddering of the engine and a change in the exhaust note. Apart from the slipping, it is unlikely that there has ever been a British locomotive that could be driven in such an almost ham-handed manner without losing time, steam, or water. Not surprisingly the dynamometer records taken in the Interchange Trials of 1948 did not flatter the Pacifics as to coal and water consumption, but they were unrivalled in their capabilities. Indeed, Cecil J. Allen said of them: 'The most uniform standard of performance throughout the tests was put up by the Southern engines, behind which it was a joy to travel.'[8]

From the driver's point of view, preparing a Pacific for service was only too easy. Instead of having to crawl inside the motion with an oilcan (a job which the more corpulent driver had to persuade or bribe his fireman to do for him), he could stand and watch whilst a fitter pumped oil into the sump; an occupation which might give him some pleasure, for there was a long-standing feud between fitters and footplatemen (probably not solely on the Southern Railway). Mechanics regarded drivers as a generally heavy-fisted body whose repair card reports were often misleading, exaggerated, or inaccurate in their diagnosis. Drivers, on the other hand, asserted that fitters did not maintain engines properly and ignored fault reports. This latter assertion took no account of a fitter's obligation to sign his statement of every job done, with the result that a subsequent failure could be traced to him; whereas a driver's transgressions could seldom be brought home. For instance, with common usage of engines, if there were flats on wheels or white metal run out of oil-starved bearings, the culprit could be any one of a dozen or so drivers, not all of whom belonged to the same running shed.

There was some difference of opinion among drivers as to the best way of driving the Bulleid Pacifics. Some preferred short cut-offs and wide open regulators, whilst others were convinced that better results were obtained with cut-offs of not less than 25%, maintaining that persistent use of shorter cut-offs caused premature knocking in the coupled axleboxes. The argument was never clearly resolved and no locomotive inspector would go so far as to lay down the law on the subject.

When new, the second batch of 'Merchant Navies' was allocated to Nine Elms, and in 1945-46, in an attempt to restore prewar standards, they were rostered as far as practicable to pairs in top-link drivers. No 35017 *Belgian Marine* was regularly driven by practitioners of the short cut-off school, and it was found that it developed axlebox knock before the others. However, axlebox knock, considered as a fault, was a relative term; for considerable clearance could develop before an engine was booked as 'unfit for fast trains'. Southern men were well used to 'King Arthurs' which, with their two big outside cylinders, developed some hammering in the driving boxes after 30,000-40,000 miles. Early cut-off was accompanied by early exhaust closure and higher compression at the end of the stroke. To reduce this and consequent knock, 'King Arthurs' were driven with not less than 25-30% cut-off.

Coupled axleboxes were handled by a specialist fitting gang at Eastleigh Works. Whilst the engine was on blocks in the erecting shops, the boxes would first be tried on the horns with the aim of securing a tight fit. Fitting the boxes was much easier with adjustable horn wedges, such as were fitted on the 'Nelsons' and 'Schools'. The object of these wedges was to make it easier for the fitter to take up the play between axlebox and horns and so prevent knock between them. For some reason Bulleid did not design his engines with wedges. There was indeed some prejudice against them because of the possibility that over-adjustment might cause a box to become solid in the horns with the consequent risk of lifting a flange over the rail-head. Great care was taken with wedge adjustment on 'Nelsons' or 'Schools' and the work was in any case entrusted to Leading Fitters. Many of the later American and French engines had wedges which were automatically adjusted by two springs of different strengths, of which the more flexible was in constant action and the stronger came into play in the exceptional case of the former's flexibility being totally absorbed. It is strange that Bulleid should not have been attracted by this automatic system.

The brakes on both classes of Pacific could land an incautious driver in trouble. The concept of the clasp brake was excellent because it provided a generous surface area of contact between the tyres and the brake shoes and avoided the one-sided pressure against wheels and axleboxes presented by the more common arrangement and the tendency of its single blocks below the wheel centres to lift weight off the springs. But there was a weakness in the Bulleid brakes in that space for the brake cylinders was limited by the room taken up by the oil bath; so that the steam brake power on the engine was nothing like as great as on a Maunsell locomotive with its large vacuum cylinders. This did not matter when working passenger trains, when the train brakes did the retarding, but when running light the drivers had to proceed with caution. There was at Nine Elms Depot a descent from the running lines into the coal stage and pit roads, where an incautious driver could find himself ramming engines taking coal with their brakes hard on. As the shedmaster's office overlooked the spot, the culprit would have another quick descent — from the footplate to the 'Guvnor's mat'!

The brake power on the six-wheel tender was likewise much inferior to that on the eight wheel tenders of the 'Nelsons', 'King Arthurs', H15s, and S15s working on the Western Section. These bogie tenders were excellent anchors when working unfitted freight trains. This was a task for which the Bulleid Pacifics, with their lack of engine brake power, were quite unsuitable — in spite of Bulleid's description of them as mixed traffic locomotives. Indeed, when working short passenger trains, no heavier than the engine, on stopping services west of Exeter and on the Somerset & Dorset line, hard braking on falling gradients would produce considerable spark-throwing from the brake-blocks. Sometimes these sparks reached the oil-soaked lagging under the casing and the smouldering material would burst into flames when the engine came to rest. To counter this, Eastleigh Works applied what became known as 'belly lagging' underneath. All 140 engines could not be protected immediately, so it was some time before the joke about having 'the firebox in the wrong place' faded away.[9]

During 1946-48 many locomotives on all the railways were converted to oil firing. Most of them had the narrow, or oblong, firebox, and on these the conversion was very successful. The equipment used was the Weir type burner, feeding from the front of the firebox, and producing a flame which circulated under and around the brick arch. This system, however, was not suited to the wide, almost square, firebox of the Bulleid boiler, as its trial on No 21C119 *Bideford* showed. 'West Country' Pacific No 21C136 *Westward Ho!* was therefore provided with a Laidlaw-Drew burner, fitted in the centre of the grate and distributing the fire with a circular motion. So equipped, the engine kept time with the 'Atlantic Coast Express'; but further trials were abandoned because the Government cancelled the oil-burning scheme and all locomotives reverted to coal.

In 1948 Bulleid caused some surprise by fitting No 35005, *Canadian Pacific*, with the American Berkley mechanical stoker. The decision was surprising because none of the 'Merchant Navy' rosters were anything like as long and arduous for the fireman as those on such services as the Anglo-Scottish expresses. The experiment did not last long, because any advantages gained were more than offset by disadvantages. Firstly, the feed screw in the tender could not cope with coal containing lumps larger than a six-inch cube, so the trials were conducted at Eastleigh mpd where the tub-loading coal stage enabled large lumps to be removed, although at the expense of time and labour; but it could not have been done at depots with hopper coaling plants. Secondly, the coal was crushed by the stoker to enable it to be blown into the firebox by steam nozzles and considerable amounts of half-burned particles were ejected at the chimney. This stuff blew back down the train, entering windows of compartments and covering restaurant car table cloths with smuts and small burn marks, causing outraged protest from passengers and restaurant car staff. Thirdly, coal consumption was above the average for even these hungry engines.

Between March and November 1952 tests were carried out at the Rugby Locomotive Testing Station and with the London Midland Region No 1 Dynamometer Car between Carlisle and Skipton with 'Merchant Navy' Pacific No 35022 *Holland America Line*. Further tests on the same engine, but with a modified chimney and blastpipe, were conducted between March and May 1953, and with a modified boiler between December 1953 and January 1954. The results were published in *British Railways Bulletin* No 10 of January 1954. The main points of the report were as follows:

1 This design of locomotive proved to be difficult to test owing to its inconsistent performance, especially with regard to power output. Not only was it often found impossible to obtain reasonable accuracy of repetitions on different occasions, but the performance would sometimes change appreciably over quite short periods of time. The changes were not usually of such magnitude as would have affected the locomotive's ability to carry out its normal duties quite effectively, but were such as to make accurate measurement exceptionally difficult.

2 On the controlled road tests the maximum steaming rate was limited to about 29,000lb/hr, which sufficed to work a train of 20 bogie coaches of 594 tons at the scheduled speeds involved, and this was the largest number of such coaches that had ever been operated over this route, and over 40% above the rostered tare load, on limited load schedules, for a Class 7 4-6-2, the most powerful locomotive normally permitted.

3 The valve gear gave rise to some difficulty in testing. It was found that the actual cut-off bore no definite or consistent relationship to the setting of the reversing gear, not only for the locomotive as a whole, but especially for the individual cylinder ends. In the shorter cut-offs particularly there was a general tendency for the actual mean cut-off to lengthen with increasing speed, but not in a smooth or regular manner. At times quite random changes occurred that appeared to be caused by minute changes of speed or boiler pressure.

4 The steam reversing gear could not be prevented by adjustment from creeping very slightly. It was modified for use during tests on the line to make fine adjustment possible, but, due to the need for continual alteration of the cut-off with changing speed, the small creep did not cause any difficulty.

5 The proneness of the locomotive to slipping whilst running (as opposed to slipping at starting) was ascribed to the fact that it could not be run for an appreciable time without lubricating oil reaching the wheel treads. This led to buckling of coupling rods which occurred on a number of occasions during the tests on the Plants and on the line.

6 During the trials on the Test Plant the locomotive demonstrated its ability to work at very high sustained rates of steaming; far higher than those at which it would normally work continuously in service. Under these conditions, however, there was a tendency for mechanical failures to occur, such as heating of coupled axleboxes, inside big ends, coupling rod bushes, etc.

7 No mechanical trouble, other than the buckled coupling rods, was experienced during the trials on the line.

The report concluded that the locomotive as designed was most effective and capable but relatively uneconomical. If operated, as these engines frequently were in service, with the reversing gear in a relatively long cut-off and with the regulator very little open, they would be still less economical, though their performance would then be more reliable mechanically and in power output. The vibration, associated with full regulator and very short cut-off working, would also be avoided.

In spite of the good draught provided by the multiple-jet blast pipe, the combustion was never very good, particularly with lower grade coal. There was, however, no evidence that the thermic syphons had anything to do with this. On the other hand there was some evidence that wider spacing of the grate bars and the provision of a deflector plate and admission of rather more air through the firehole with the doors closed would effect some improvement. The draughting arrangement could almost certainly be improved by some re-design of the chimney. The actual choke was located about seven inches above the effective choke where the vacuum is the highest.

One locomotive of the class had been in service for some time with a special blastpipe, having a single circular orifice, and a chimney of reduced diameter. A similar chimney, adjustable vertically in the smokebox, and two blastpipes with different orifice diameters were supplied for trials. With this class of locomotive the essence of the problem was that the height available between the top of the inside valve chest and the top of the chimney, as limited by the loading gauge, was very restricted. It was not possible, therefore, to obtain good proportions for the parts because the various requirements were conflicting. In spite of every effort to obtain good combustion, none of the combinations of blastpipe and chimney gave results that were up to the standard set by the multiple-jet arrangement, and none of them enabled the boiler to produce an amount of steam comparable to that produced with the multiple jet exhaust. The trials in fact showed that a satisfactory compromise between the conflicting requirements is impossible in the reduced height available, as good single blastpipe and chimney would need about a foot more. On these locomotives the use of the multiple jet was practically unavoidable if anything like full use was to be made of the steaming capacity of the boiler when the coal was inferior.

Modifying the boiler by removing the thermic syphons necessitated a completely different type of brick arch, and any differences observed might have been due as much to the different arch as to the absence of the syphons. Without the syphons, however, the locomotive was certainly much more difficult to fire correctly than it had been formerly. Whilst it would not be worthwhile, on boiler performance grounds alone, to remove the syphons, it seemed equally not worthwhile to fit them in any British coal-fired locomotive of similar or smaller size. An appreciable advantage in improved steam consumption would, however, normally be expected from the higher superheat that results from the removal of the syphons.

The report deals only, of course, with matters affecting the performance of the locomotive and not with its maintenance; but taking these two aspects together it is apparent that, having regard to the capabilities of these Pacifics, a decision to rebuild both classes could not be unexpected.

In 1962 No 34064 *Fighter Command* was fitted with a Giesl ejector, but as the steaming of the Bulleid Pacifics was already excellent, there was no particular improvement. A Riddles Standard '9F' 2-10-0 was also tested with this equipment at Derby Works under arrangements made by R. C. Bond, but, as he had predicted, the results did not justify its adoption.[10]

One might suitably conclude from this chapter on the unrebuilt Pacifics by the following passage from a letter to the Author from S. C. Townroe:

'When I became Running Shed Superintendent at Eastleigh in 1947 the depot was threatened with an allocation of the ever-growing number of Pacifics. Not wanting to develop grey hairs prematurely, I had an idea. The "Lord Nelsons" were no longer wanted at Nine Elms or Stewarts Lane, and as they needed a bit of knowing by enginemen and boiler smiths, my suggestion that all 16 should be re-allocated to Eastleigh for working top-link duties was accepted, so Eastleigh mpd only suffered the Pacifics when ex-Works on trial, and did not have to maintain any!.'

Notes

1 Bradley, D. L.; *Locomotives of the Southern Railway Part 2*; London, The Railway Correspondence & Travel Society, 1976, pp58ff
2 Bulleid, H. A. V.; *Bulleid of the Southern*; London, Ian Allan Ltd, 1977, p86
3 *ibid*
4 Townroe, S. C.; information to the Author
5 Bulleid, *op cit*, p65
6 Memorandum to the Mechanical Engineering Assistant, Brighton
7 Townroe, *op cit*
8 Allen, Cecil J.; *The Locomotive Exchanges*; London, Ian Allan, 1950, p172
9 Townroe, *op cit*
10 Bond, R. C.; information to the Author

Above left: The first of the 'Light Pacifics' No 21C101 *Exeter*. *IAL*

Left: No 21C101 *Exeter* with an up Ilfracombe–Exeter train at Braunton in 1945. A rare early picture of one of these engines in service in the West Country. *C. B. Harley*

Above: Both the front and rear of Bulleid Pacifics carried electric lighting for route indication at night. The tender was so equipped for working tender first. *Both BR*

Right: No 21C154 *Lord Beaverbrook* on a down boat train near Chislehurst.
Wethersett Collection/IAL

GOLDEN
ARROW
3
21C135

GOLDEN
ARROW
4
21C157

Far left, top: 'West Country' No 21C135 as yet unnamed on the 'Golden Arrow' service. *IAL*

Far left, bottom: Sydenham Hill on 25 June 1949 as 'Battle of Britain' No 21C157 passes with the 'Golden Arrow'.
Wethersett Collection/IAL

Above: As yet unnamed No 21C162 is seen with experimental turned-in smoke deflectors.
Crown Copyright, National Railway Museum

Left: No 21C164, later *Fighter Command* is seen in photographic shop grey livery in July 1947.
Crown Copyright, National Railway Museum

Top: The up 'Arrow' passing Folkestone Warren on 5 July 1949, headed by 'Battle of Britain' class No 34083. *T. H. Watts*

Above: No 34085 *501 Squadron* backs the empty stock for the 'Golden Arrow' past Stewarts Lane motive power depot, en route for Victoria. *R. C. Riley*

Right: Due to engineering works at Victoria, the 'Arrow' was diverted on 31 January and is seen passing Penshurst on the Redhill–Tonbridge line hauled by No 34085 *501 Squadron*. *D. Cross*

Below: The up 'Arrow' headed by No 34085 *501 Squadron* in May 1959 passing Chart Sidings, near Ashford. *J. C. Beckett*

GOLDEN
ARROW
PENSHURST

Top right: No 34072 *257 Squadron* stands complete with headboard ready to work the 'Night Ferry' at Stewarts lane mpd. *IAL*

Centre right: No 21C119 (later *Bideford*) stands alongside Romney, Hythe and Dymchurch Railway No 5 *Hercules*, which is arriving at Ashford Works for overhaul in March 1946. *IAL*

Below: No 21C105 *Barnstaple* as fitted with indicator shelter for test purposes. *H. M. Madgwick*

Far right, top: No S21C146 and 21C114 stand at Exmouth Junction shed in April 1949. No S21C146 carries both this number and BR No 34046. *A. J. Book*

Far right, bottom: 'West Country' No 21C113 passing alongside the seawall at Teignmouth on 26 September 1946. This was one of the exchange GWR/SR turns between Exeter and Plymouth. *B. A. Butt*

34046
S 21C146
SOUTHERN
21C114

21C113

SOUTHERN
21C138

SOUTHERN
6
6
21C133

Above left: Sydenham Hill with No 21C138 on an up Continental boat train.
Wethersett Collection/IAL

Left: Sydenham Hill with No 21C133 on a down Continental boat train.
Wethersett Collection/IAL

Above: No 21C158 at Bournemouth Central in May 1947. *G. O. P. Pearce*

Right: A contrast in front ends, as Nos 863 *Lord Rodney* and 21C160 stand on adjacent roads at Waterloo on 20 March 1948.
C. C. B. Herbert

Below right: No 21C163 on the 11.35 Victoria-Ramsgate service on Sole Street Bank.
B. A. Rewes

Above: No 21C168 *Kenley.*
BR

Above right: No 34048 *Crediton* heads the 5.45pm Ilfracombe-Barnstaple stopping train (made up of WR stock) near Morthoe station on 30 June 1950.
A. F. Taylor

Right: The 'Thanet Belle' headed by No 21C157 *Biggin Hill* near Chislehurst.
Wethersett Collection/IAL

34048
THE
THANET BELLE

Right: A closer view of the smoke deflectors on No 34006 ***Bude.*** *M. J. Esau*

Below: The down 'Kentish Belle' passing Bromley South during the summer of 1954 headed by No 34017 ***Ilfracombe.*** *R. Russell*

Left: No 34035 *Shaftesbury,* with a modified front end arrangement, a later effort to help stop the smoke from clinging to the casing. *IAL*

Below: No 34029 *Lundy* on an up Bideford meat train waiting for the road at Cowley Bridge junction, Exeter on 16 July 1958. *R. C. Riley*

34038

Above left: No 34103 *Calstock* is coaled by crane at Bournemouth mpd in June 1965.
P. L. Simpson

Far left: Working tender first is No 34091 *Weymouth* with the Sunday 15.50 Yeovil (Town)-Yeovil Junction, where it will run round its train before proceeding to Waterloo on 23 June 1963. *G. D. King*

Left: The 18.30 Waterloo-Bournemouth service on 6 June 1966 will depart as soon as No 34038 *Lynton* gets a grip on the rails, sanding at Waterloo was banned for fear of insulating the track circuiting system.
M. S. Stokes

Above: No 34006 *Bude* stands at Bath mpd, while No 34057 *Biggin Hill* is turned, during the course of a farewell rail tour over the Somerset & Dorset line. *D. A. Idle*

Centre right: No 34094 *Mortehoe* is seen backing into Doncaster station, prior to returning southward with a Warwickshire Railway Society special. Also in the photograph is an 'A1' an 'A3' and a 'K1'.
M. Fowler

Bottom right: No 34033 *Chard* on the down 'Thanet Belle', on Christmas Eve 1948.
P. Ransome-Wallis

Top left: ***Chard*** **again, on the 14.50 Plymouth Friary-Waterloo near Mannamead on 15 July 1956, when single line working was in force between Laira and Plymouth North Road.** *R. C. Riley*

Centre left: There is just about room for No 34041 ***Wilton*** **inside Branksome shed in 1953.** *IAL*

Below: Light Pacifics Nos 34092, 34102, 34067 and 34090 leaving Watford junction to turn on the Watford High Street turntable after working hockey specials to Wembley Central, 10 March 1956. *J. N. Faulkner*

Right: No 34098 ***Templecombe*** **departing from Hailsham with a two-coach local to Eastbourne: this formed part of a diagram covering a heavy Oxted line commuter train.** *IAL*

Below right: A contrast in front ends, 'Battle of Britain' No 34059 ***Sir Archibald Sinclair,*** **alongside ex-LNER 'BI' 4-6-0 No 61058.** *C. C. B. Herbert*

34098
THE NORFOLKMAN
34059
61058

WINSTON CHURCHILL
34051

Above left: No 34064 *Fighter Command* on an up boat train at Hildenborough in September 1949.
E. R. Wethersett/IAL

Left: No 34051 *Winston Churchill* at Eastleigh on 2 July 1964, behind is No 34073 *249 Squadron,* 'Q1' No 33033 and a Standard Class 5 while in the background lurk two Maunsell Moguls and a 'Q', with some of the 'new order' Class 33s. *J. R. Carter*

Above: 'Super power' for the 16.35 Bath–Templecombe local on 14 August 1960, headed by No 34043 *Combe Martin* leaving Midford.
Derek Cross

Centre right: Clapham Junction with Giesl ejector fitted No 34064 *Fighter Command* shunting the yard.
J. Scrace

Bottom right: Near Hamble Halt, No 34057 *Biggin Hill* heads the 11.30 Brighton–Plymouth service on 25 July 1963. *J. Scrace*

Above: No 34075 later *246 Squadron* at the head of a down boat train, near Wandsworth Road. *IAL*

Left: No 34099 *Lynmouth* on the 13.55 Brighton-Victoria crossing Riddlesdown Viaduct.

Below left: In November 1955 No 34090 *Sir Eustace Missenden Southern Railway* leaves Weston-super-Mare General station at the head of an SR originating special. *S. C. Nash*

Above right: No 34076 later *41 Squadron,* note the space left in the lining out for the nameplate. *LPC*

Right: Two trains on the same line? The scene at Faversham with No 34076 *41 Squadron* on a Ramsgate-Victoria express and a 'DI' 4-4-0 No 31545 on a Dover-Faversham local, stopped by signals. *A. W. V. Mace*

RITISH RAILWAYS
34076
34076

Above: Returned to Nine Elms shed after working a special No 34057 *Biggin Hill* rests, the lighting shows up the unevenness of the air-smoothed casing. *V. C. K. Allen*

Left: Ilfracombe station on 18 May 1959 with No 34072 *257 Squadron* marshalling empty stock *K. L. Cook*

Below left: The 10.30 Waterloo-Weymouth passing Worgret junction with the branch for Swanage diverting to the right. No 34063 *279 Squadron* is in charge on 30 May 1950. *H. C. Flemons*

Above right: An informal shot of Nine Elms loco yard, the Pacific has a drink while the driver lights up a cigarette. *Eric Treacy*

Right: Nine Elms mpd with No 34066 *Spitfire*, resting between duties. *Eric Treacy*

37

7P 5FA
34066
BRITISH
RAILWAYS

Top: No 34073 *249 Squadron* leaving Ashford with an up freight train on 15 June 1960; by this time dieselisation was starting to displace the Pacifics from SE Division workings. *D. C. Ovenden*

Above: A down Continental express approaching Ashford station headed by No 34089 *602 Squadron* in July 1959. *D. C. Ovenden*

Right: No 34101 *Hartland* winding round the Petts Wood spur with a Victoria-Dover boat train in April 1957. *A. R. Butcher*

Below: The 13.30 Victoria-Folkestone boat train is hauled by 34083 *605 Squadron,* near Shortlands on 13 September 1958. *C. Hogg*

34101
130

Top left: No 34018 *Axminster* on the 09.20 Waterloo-Bournemouth excursion climbing the 1 in 60 to Medstead & Four Marks, 'over the Alps' as the route between Alton and Winchester was known to the railway staff, owing to engineering works in Farnham in May 1955. *L. Elsey*

Centre left: No 34006 *Bude* on an up Southampton boat special at Worting junction flyover in September 1951. *M. W. Earley*

Below: No 34023 *Blackmore Vale* with the up 'Royal Wessex' at Brockenhurst on 3 December 1966. This locomotive is now preserved on the Bluebell Railway. *P. J. Fowler*

Right: With a train of track ballast from Meldon Quarry in tow No 34076 *41 Squadron* nears Crediton on 4 September 1964. *R. W. Hawkins*

Below right: The 15.00 Ilfracombe-Waterloo draws away from Barnstaple Junction behind No 34061 *73 Squadron* with Ivatt Class 2 No 41295 on shed. *K. L. Cook*

34061

PULLMAN
34088

34004

Above: As yet unnamed, No 34074 with the down 'Golden Arrow' near Bickley on 8 August 1949. *R. W. Beaton*

Left: No 34004 *Yeovil* on the SR's North Cornwall line approaching St Kew Highway with a down stopping train. *B. A. Butt*

Below: The Emperor of Ethiopia visited Britain in October 1954 and a 'Battle of Britain' was allocated for Royal Train duty, No 34088 *213 Squadron* has been cleared to perfection, complete with whitened wheel rims, and polished buffers for the journey between Portsmouth and Victoria on 14 October 1954. *BR*

Top left: No 34088 sets out from Portsmouth & Southsea. *Pursey C. Short*

34051
34051

34051

Above left: Another special working allocated to a Bulleid Pacific was that of Sir Winston Churchill's funeral train. No 34051 *Winston Churchill* is seen in ex-works condition.

Left: The special funeral train conveying the body of Sir Winston Churchill and family mourners from Waterloo to Handborough is seen shortly after passing Virginia Water at speed, hauled by No 34051 *Winston Churchill* on 30 January 1965. This locomotive is preserved as one of the National Collection and is at present at Didcot Railway Centre. *Brian Stephenson*

Above: The crew of this Pacific pose for the photographer. Note how the lining is carried round the cab sheets. *IAL*

Above right: The single chimney of 'Merchant Navy' No 35019 is seen to advantage in this photograph taken from Wareham footbridge; as are the three safety valves mounted on the boiler barrel. *B. Knowlman*

Right: 'Merchant Navy' No 21C14 *Nederland Line* receives a boiler washout, note the hole in the cab sides for the washout hose to go through. *IAL*

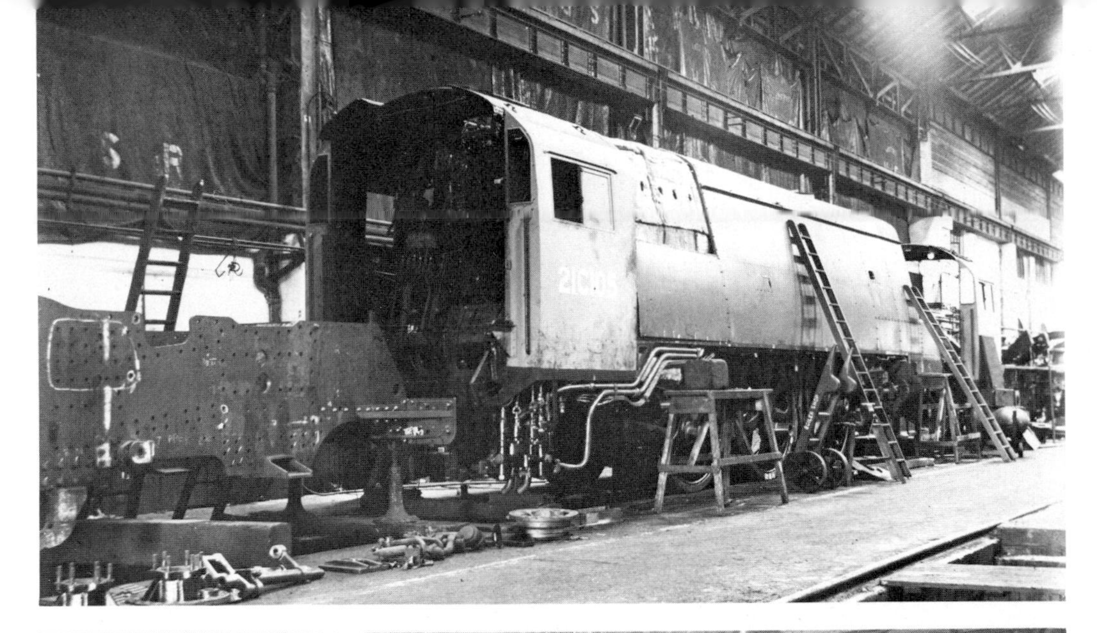

Above right: No 21C105, later *Barnstaple* is seen here under construction in Brighton Works in 1945. *IAL*

Right: No 34038 *Lynton* is seen here under repair at Eastleigh Works in July 1953. *R. H. Clark*

Below: No 35010 stored at Bournemouth Central prior to entry to Eastleigh Works to be rebuilt. *C. P. Boocock*

Above: No 34023 *Blackmore Vale* at Corfe Castle on the Swanage branch on a LCGB excursion on 7 May 1967, two months before the end of SR steam. *Derek Cross*

Left: The works of a Bulleid Pacific, seen here under construction at Brighton, the 'chain-driven' valve gear can clearly be seen to the right of the connecting rod. The shafts either side are from the weighshaft which is connected to the steam reverser. The expansion links can also be seen between the frame stretchers. It was to remove this arrangement and improve reliability that the engines were rebuilt.
Crown Copyright, National Railway Museum

6
Rebuilding

On 24 April 1953 the crank axle of 'Merchant Navy' class No 35020 *Bibby Line* broke when the engine was running at speed with the 4.30pm Exeter-Waterloo express, near Crewkerne. Luckily *Bibby Line* was not derailed. The fault in the axle was due to fretting corrosion at the point where the chain wheel was clamped to the driving axle close to the right hand crank web. The presence of the chain wheel at that point caused a stress at a critical place near the web. It indicated, too, that the chain wheel was taking more than the 1.5hp that Bulleid had claimed was all that was needed to drive his Bulleid-Walschaerts valve gear. R. A. Riddles, Member of the Railway Executive for Mechanical & Electrical Engineering, directed that all the 'Merchant Navies' were to be withdrawn from service and an examination carried out. The axles of seven other 'Merchant Navies' were found to have slight fractures and a start was made immediately on examining the axles of the 'West Countries' and eight of these were found to be faulty.

Broken crank axles were a weak point during the early years of the steam locomotive and had led to some serious accidents; but this weakness had been largely overcome by improvements in design and metallurgy, and by the 1950s such incidents were regarded as a thing of the past. A crank axle failure on one of the most modern of express engines therefore caused considerable alarm, and thereafter regular checks for flawed axles by ultrasonic equipment were adopted by British Railways.

Riddles had already decided that the Bulleid Pacifics should be rebuilt and plans were being prepared.[1] In these plans a modification was made to the attachment of the chain driving sprocket (which had been a factor in the failure) on all the Pacifics (see the letter below to the Author from R. G. Jarvis). The crank axles otherwise were strong enough and needed no alteration.

The Chief Mechanical & Electrical Engineer, Southern Region, issued in January 1955 a *Report on the Proposed Modifications to the 'Merchant Navy' and 'West Country' Classes of Locomotives*. One particularly interesting feature of the report was its disclosure that the tests mentioned in *Bulletin No 10* were carried out in comparison with a 'Britannia' class Pacific. The following is a summary of the main points of the report:

Design

The locomotives embodied a number of design features not usually employed in British locomotive practice, including a special valve gear with a chain drive, an oil bath enclosing three sets of special valve gear and the inside motion, a smokebox of irregular shape, and a special casing over the whole of the upper part of the locomotive.

Performance

When hauling the principal expresses of the Region, these locomotives had demonstrated their ability to run to time, with an ample margin of power, due to their excellent steaming properties and free running characteristics. In availability and maintenance, however, they were less satisfactory, whilst their consumption of coal, water and oil was high in comparison with other locomotives. These unsatisfactory features could be covered under the following four headings: running costs, reliability, availability, and cost of repair and maintenance.

Below: 'Merchant Navy' Pacific as rebuilt at Eastleigh, in 1956-1959. The 'West Country' Pacifics were rebuilt along similar lines at Eastleigh, 1957-1961.

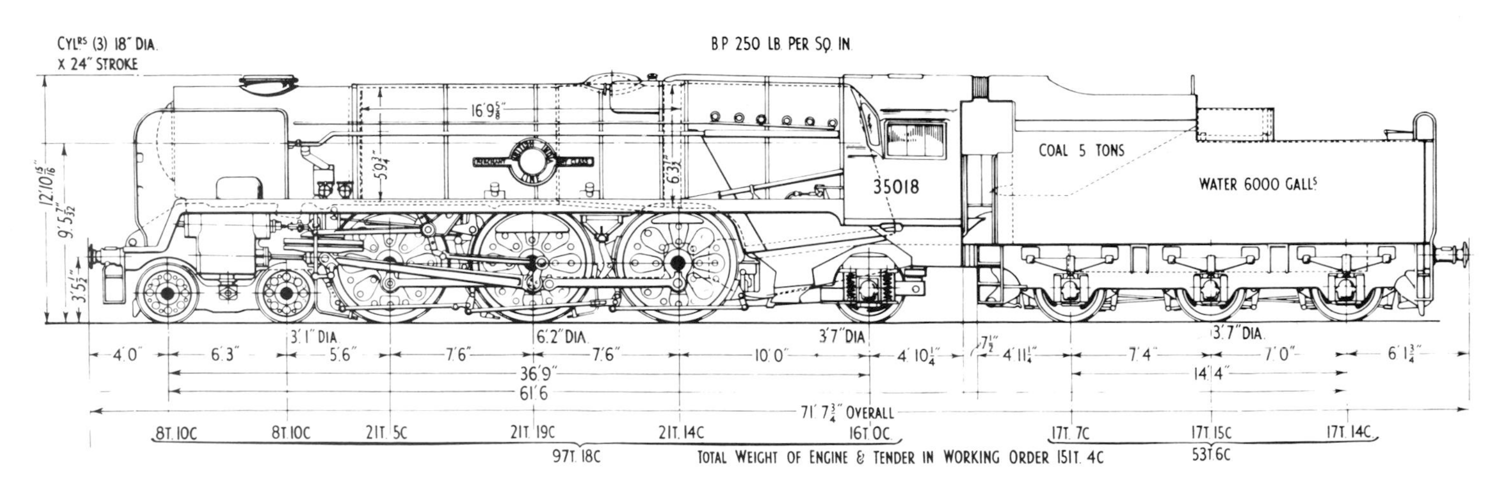

1 Running costs

(a) Thermal efficiency — Tests were conducted in 1951 and 1952 at Rugby and on the road between Carlisle and Skipton with 'Merchant Navy' No 35022 and a BR Class 7 Pacific. There was no substantial difference in boiler efficiency between the two classes (the actual boiler efficiency of the 'Merchant Navy' in standard condition was only 1.5% less than that of the Class 7), but the cylinder efficiency of the 'Merchant Navy' showed to a disadvantage over a wide range of working. This covered light working (a steam rate of 14,000), normal working (20,000), and very heavy working (28,000lb of steam per hour), each at speeds of 20, 40, and 60mph. In all tests but one the 'Merchant Navy' showed a percentage reduction of efficiency as compared with the 'Britannia' of from 8.7% to 18.5%. The sole exception was very heavy working at 20mph when the two engines were equal. This lower efficiency was ascribed primarily to be inefficient utilisation of the steam in the cylinders of the 'Merchant Navy' due to the faulty distribution of the steam by the valves.

(b) Coal — Again, at various drawbar horsepower figures at 60 and 40mph respectively the consumption of the 'Merchant Navy' was in all but one instance from 8.6% to 17.5% higher than that of the 'Britannia'. In the one instance they were equal. The high coal consumption of the 'Merchant Navy' was similarly shown in the 1948 Interchange Trials. The 'West Country' class locomotive on these trials had a particularly high coal consumption due to the absence of damper doors to the ashpan; for very skilful handling by the fireman was necessary to avoid blowing off.

(c) Water — The water consumption of a locomotive gives a measure of the cylinder efficiency, and for any similar degree of superheat it is approximately true that the cylinder efficiency and the water per indicated horsepower are inversely proportional. The trials between Carlisle and Skipton showed that on the above-mentioned tests the 'Merchant Navy' had a consumption superior to that of the 'Britannia' by from 4.1% to 16.7%. These figures again agreed approximately with those obtained from the Interchange Trials.

(d) Oil — In practice it had been found virtually impossible to make the oil bath oiltight. The net result of leakage from the oil bath was that, over a typical period of 18 months, the average consumption of high quality lubricating oil amounted to just over 16 pints per 100 miles per engine in addition to the 15 pints of engine and cylinder oil per 100 miles issued to enginemen and artisan staffs — a total of 31 pints. This compared with the 9.5 pints per 100 miles issued to a 'Lord Nelson' class for all purposes.

2 Reliability

As a result of investigation into troubles and failures which have occurred with these locomotives, modifications had been introduced which had tended to improve their reliability. The principal features which had made them unreliable were the valve gear, the oil bath, the air-smoothed casing, the smokebox and leading end, and the rocking grate on the 'West Country' class.

(a) Valve gear — Failure was not infrequent and the principal causes were fracture of the rocker shafts, fracture of the driving chains, and damage to the valves due to over-travel.

(b) Oil bath — The oil bath, apart from requiring constant attention by topping up, made maintenance more difficult as the big end and valve gear parts could not be readily examined. It was also very difficult to exclude water and this caused appreciable corrosion on the motion parts.

(c) Air-smoothed casing — Fires on orthodox locomotives were practically unknown, but 38 cases were reported in 1953 on 'Merchant Navy' and 'West Country' classes. Most of the fires began near the ashpan hopper doors, due to the accumulation of oil-soaked inflammable matter, and frequently spread to the boiler lagging plates and clothing. The shape of the casing tended to trap heat from the engine and set up temperatures approximately of the same order as the flash point of the oil, so that once a fire started combustion could proceed readily under the casing, forming a furnace. The air-smoothed casing was troublesome to maintain and parts needing attention were generally hidden so that removal of parts of the casing was often necessary.

(d) Smokebox and leading end of the locomotive — The frames had behaved well; the only trouble being at the leading end of the 'West Country' class, at the front of the inside cylinder. Frame distortion gave rise to trouble with the main steam pipes in the smokebox, causing leakage which had a detrimental effect on the steaming.

(e) Rocking grate on the 'West Country' class — On account of its unreliability the rocking grate was little used in the manner intended, because it could collapse after either rocking or fire-dropping.

3 Availability

The number of weekdays out of service during 1952 for the following three classes were: 'Merchant Navy' 61.69; 'West Country' 53.95; Lord Nelson' 49.38.

4 Cost of repair and maintenance

The cost of repair in pence per engine mile (to the nearest penny) for three classes of Southern Region locomotives, three of the Eastern & North Eastern Regions, and one of the LMR, were SR 'Merchant Navy' 14; 'West Country' 12, 'Lord Nelson' 11; E&NER 'A1' 7, 'A4' 10, 'A2/3' 9; LMR 'Coronation' 10. In addition, in the Works considerably more man-hours were required for intermediate and general repairs to the 'Merchant Navy' and 'West Country' class locomotives then for any other locomotives of approximately comparable size and power. The cost of intermediate and general repairs to engines and tenders (excluding boilers) was 20% more for these two classes than for 'Lord Nelsons'.

Proposal to modify the locomotives

Three 'Merchant Navy' and three 'West Country' class locomotives had been modified recently in a number of respects, and some improvement had been shown. The proposals now put forward would virtually eliminate the principal troublesome features and would bring the running costs into line with those of the other leading express passenger locomotives without impairing their performance in any way, whilst increasing their availability and reducing their maintenance. The proposals involved the retention of the boiler, frames, outside cylinders, wheels, axleboxes, etc, and the replacement or removal of the special valve gear with its rocker shafts, the inside cylinder, the smokebox, the superheater header, the steampipes etc, the reversing gear, the piston heads and rods, the oil bath, the air-smoothed casing, the mechanical lubricators, the regulator, the ashpan and grate, the cylinder cocks, and the sandboxes; whilst on the tender the raves, the tank sieves, the water level gauge, and the intermediate drawbar would be replaced or removed.

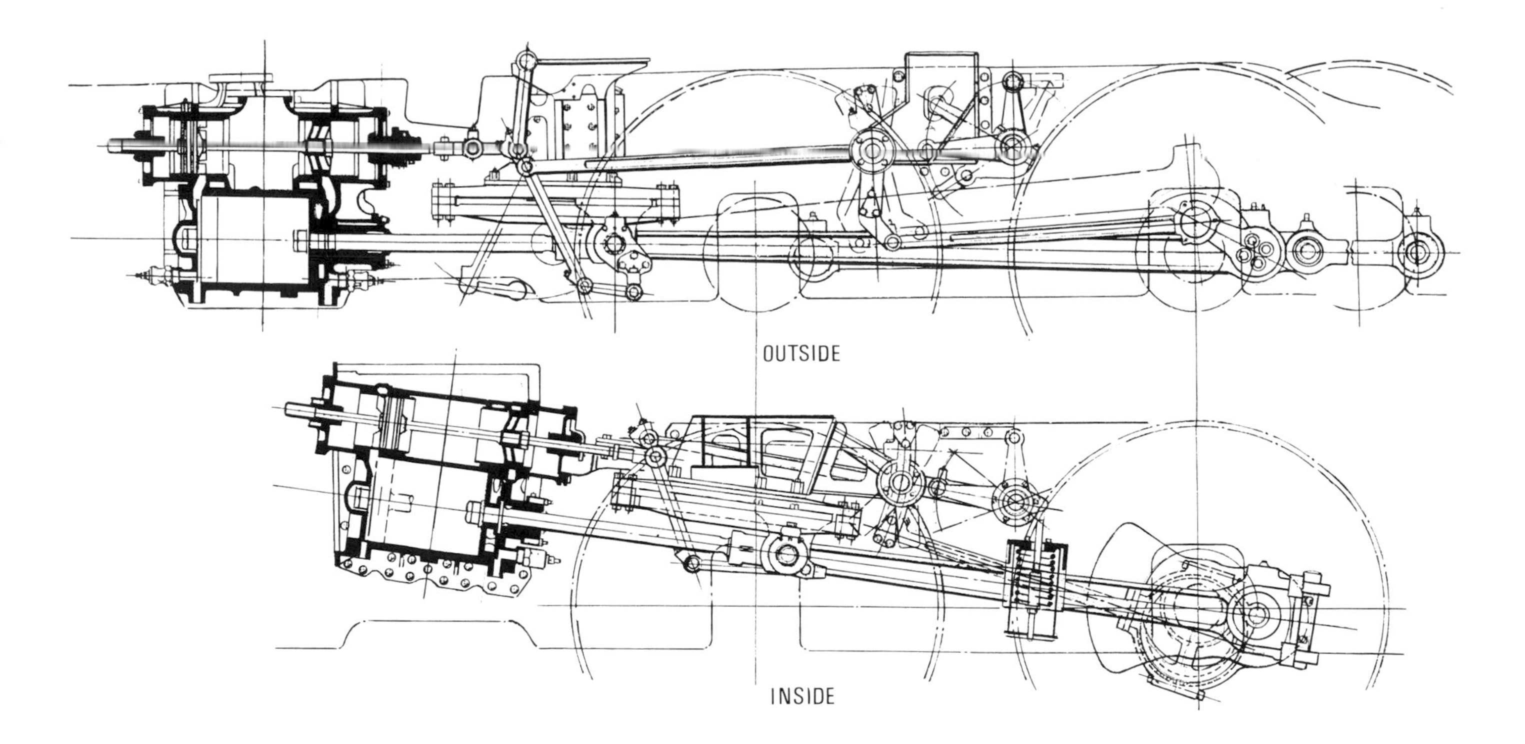

Above: Diagram showing the Walschaerts valve gear arrangement as fitted to the rebuilt locomotives.

The main points governing the design of the components that would replace those listed above were as follows:

1 Valve gear

The purpose was to provide the locomotive with three independent sets of Walschaerts valve gear. The two outside sets would be similar to those of the Standard Class 4 2-6-4 tank engines and the inside gear would follow the design of the Southern Region 'Schools' class. Two new driving crank pins would be provided to take the return cranks. An eccentric would be placed on the crank axle in place of the existing chain-driven sprocket. (Provision was made for this latter modification when the crank axle was redesigned following upon the failures in 1953.)

2 Inside cylinder

Forward of the inside cylinder (which would have a piston valve with inside admission) and bolted to it, would be a saddle. These two components would butt up to the existing stretchers and give a very strong construction which would eliminate the frame fractures experienced at the leading end of the 'West Country' class.

3 Smokebox, superheater header, and steam pipes

A circular smokebox, fixed to the saddle, would ensure a robust construction and remove the troubles experienced with the existing design of steam pipes and stuffing boxes. A new header would be needed to suit the circular smokebox, but the existing smokebox door would be retained.

4 Reversing Gear

The reversing gear would consist of one shaft for both inside and outside valve gears, operated by means of a screw. This would enable fine adjustment to the cut-off and would result in the locomotives being worked at an early cut-off with a degree of certainty not possible with the steam reversing gear.

5 Piston heads and rods

The existing type of piston heads with a coned attachment to the piston rod would be replaced by parallel-fastened heads of the type used on BR Standard locomotives. A good deal of trouble had been experienced in the past due to piston heads becoming loose.

6 Oil bath

The elimination of the oil bath would make it much easier to examine the inside big end and the trouble experienced with rusting pins and gear would cease. It would also help to keep the underside of the locomotive clean and stop slipping due to oil getting on to the wheel treads.

7 Boiler clothing

Normal type of clothing would be fitted to the boiler which, together with the removal of the oil bath, would stop fires breaking out on oil-saturated boiler clothing mattresses. In addition, pipework and other fittings would be more accessible. Footplating would be provided along the side of the engine.

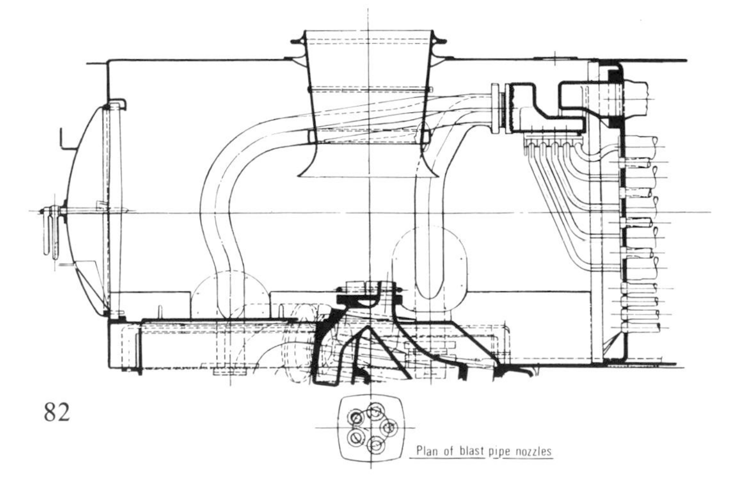

Left: Diagram of smokebox of a rebuilt Pacific showing the draughting arrangement.

8 Mechanical lubricators

Two new mechanical lubricators would be used for lubrication of the cylinders and axleboxes and would be mounted at suitable positions on the motion brackets.

9 Regulator

The existing regulator would be replaced by one of the horizontal grid type, arranged in such a way as to give a well-graduated opening in order to reduce the tendency of the locomotives to slip.

10 Ashpan and grate

Both classes of locomotive would be fitted with new ashpans, having hopper bottom doors and front and rear damper doors.

11 Cylinder cocks

The existing coned plug type of cylinder cock had proved expensive to maintain and the poppet type would be fitted in its place.

12 Sandboxes

New sandboxes would be provided and fitted, where possible, between the frames.

13 Tender

Raves on the tender sides would be removed and tunnels provided for fire irons. Sieves, located in boxes mounted external to the tank (following the design on BR locomotives), would replace the existing unsatisfactory strainers. The existing water level indicator was of primitive design and unsatisfactory; it would be replaced by the BR type. Over 90% of the intermediate drawbars had been found defective on entering Works. This was due to two unsatisfactory features, and the drawgear would be modified.

Programme for the Conversion of the Locomotives

It was proposed that the 30 'Merchant Navy' class locomotives should first be modified, followed by the 110 'West Country' class. Drawings could be prepared in time for 6 'Merchant Navy' class locomotives to be modified during 1955, and after that 24 could be dealt with each year until all the Pacifics had been rebuilt by 1961. It would then be possible to save 10 Grade 1 fitters and 17 fitters' assistants. The Regional Accountant estimated that the whole cost of conversion of the 'Merchant Navy' class would be recovered by 1962, and of the 'West Country' class by 1966.[2]

The report thus included a restrained and simplified narrative of the events which had led to the submission of the proposals, and it left a good deal to be read between the lines. More lurid accounts of troubles on the road and in the Running Sheds had already been circulated amongst locomotive engineers throughout British Railways. These at first had an incredulous reception, but the report of course confirmed them.

Approval for the conversion of the Bulleid Pacifics was given, but initially for only 30 of either class during 1955 and 1956. The reason for limiting the number was that the recent Modernisation Plan for British Railways envisaged a change of motive power from steam to diesel or electric. Recommendations for the rebuilding of the remaining locomotives were to be submitted from year to year.

Before the first 'Merchant Navy' had been modified, however, there was a serious failure with No 35016 *Elders Fyffes* on 16 November 1955 at Gillingham, Dorset, when all four coupling rods broke at speed, and the bronze driving axleboxes were badly cracked — one of them being completely broken. Having regard to previous troubles with the coupling rods, it was obvious that they would also have to be redesigned and it was decided to replace the expensive bronze boxes with cast steel ones. These two modifications were therefore added to the list.

The plans for the modification of the locomotives were prepared by R. G. Jarvis, Chief Technical Adviser (Locomotives) SR, under the general direction of the CM&EE SR, in consultation with the CME, BR, R. C. Bond (R. A. Riddles having by this time retired).

In a letter to the Author, Jarvis wrote:

'We had to give a good deal of thought to the most economical way of eliminating the troublesome features whilst retaining other features such as the boiler and chassis, which were in most respects excellent. The basic scheme was to dispense with the chain-driven valve gear and oil bath and the air-smooth casing. We used BR standard parts wherever possible, but did not replace any more than was strictly necessary to effect the desired improvements in performance and reliability.

'It was found possible to retain the outside cylinders by adapting a fairly standard Walschaerts valve gear to outside admission and using new steamchest covers with United Kingdom cast iron packings, which had already been used very successfully on the Southern Region. Actually the valve gear was based on that for the BR 2-6-4 tank locomotives, which were also designed at Brighton.

'For the inside cylinder a new steel casting was provided, as the steamchest had to be moved over from the centre line of the cylinder to the right hand side, so as to be in line with the Walschaerts valve gear. As this was a completely new inside 'engine', standard practice was followed using inside admission. This at least made high pressure valve spindle packings unnecessary, where access would have been more difficult.

'The Walschaerts valve gear was very straightforward and did not present us with any specially difficult problems. Possibly head-room was available because the tapering of the boiler was on the underside, sloping upwards to the smokebox, and it was virtually horizontal at the top ie the reverse of Churchward's taper boiler).

'The only unusual feature was the attachment of the single eccentric to the RH crank sweep by means of a spigot and five studs. This modification was also applied to the unrebuilt engines for the attachment of the chain-driven sprocket; the original clamped-on fitting having been a factor in axle fatigue failure. When this modification was introduced the plans for rebuilding were well advanced and the opportunity was taken to prepare the crank axles beforehand to receive their eccentrics. This also ensured that the pairs of driving wheels were reasonably interchangeable between rebuilt and unrebuilt locomotives. (The outside crankpins, however, were not standard.)

'I suppose that locomotives with three cylinders, all driving on the second pair of coupled wheels and having three independent sets of Walschaerts valve gear are rare, but Stanier's 3-cylinder 2-6-4 tank for the Tilbury section is a precedent.

'Certainly the rebuilt Bulleid Pacifics behaved very well, and Sam Ell, who conducted the test of No 35020, told me that they were the most predictable engines he had ever tested (praise indeed from Swindon). I am afraid that Mr Bulleid never quite forgave me.'

At a meeting in the Eastleigh Locomotive Works Manager's office on 1 April 1955,[3] it was announced that locomotives would be rebuilt when they became due for major overhaul, and that provided the new parts were ready, the work could be done without interrupting the day-to-day flow of repairs. On the basis of two Pacific major overhauls a month, it should be possible to carry through the alterations at that rate. The designs for the modifications were not yet, however, complete, and it was unlikely that much material would be ready for at least six months. In view of this it might not be possible to complete the first locomotive before the end of 1955.

On 16 June the Locomotive Works Managers at Eastleigh, Ashford and Brighton were informed of the CM&EE's intention to modify 15 'Merchant Navy' class locomotives first, because of the urgent need to improve their availability, and to follow them with 15 'West Country' class.[4] It was subsequently decided that the first modified engine should be ready by the first week in January. Working on the Eastleigh repair schedule of 28 days, it was announced that the engine selected would have to be in Eastleigh Works by 30 November. However, this timing was hastily amended the following day to 15 November, because Eastleigh had made the almost laughable error of working on a calendar month instead of 28 working days! As the various components had also been requested for the original date, the delivery of these too had to be brought forward.[5] In the event, even 15 November proved too optimistic, probably largely because the details of reconstruction were as yet unfamiliar, and it was 9 February before the rebuilt No 35018 *British India Line* left the Erecting Shop at Eastleigh.

An interesting minor problem of the rebuilding is shown by a letter from Jarvis on 15 May 1956 to the Works Manager, Eastleigh, about the necessary alteration to nameplates for the modified 'West Country' and 'Battle of Britain' engines. He sent two sketches showing a typical arrangement for each type and asked that wooden mock-ups should be set up on already modified 'Merchant Navy' class locomotives to enable to decision to be made. The mock-ups were to consist of two pieces of plywood cut to the shapes in the sketches with plaques and nameplates temporarily fixed on them from suitable 'West Country' and 'Battle of Britain' class engines in the Shops. As the length of the nameplates varied considerably the longest plates available should be used.[6]

The second engine to be rebuilt was No 35020 *Bibby Line*, which was completed in April 1956. The following month *Bibby Line* was prepared for comparative trials by having its modified tender replaced by one with high side sheeting to facilitate the attachment of the dynamometer car cables. The trials took place in June 1956 and the results were described in the British Transport Commission *Bulletin No 20* of 1958. The tests were carried out and the Bulletin was prepared by the CM&EE Department of the Western Region in conjunction with the CM&EE Department of the Southern Region and under the auspices of the Locomotive Testing Joint Sub-Committee.

In extenuation of the locomotives in their original condition, it was stated that although they had given sterling service and demonstrated their ability to run to time, with an ample margin of power, due to their excellent steaming capabilities and free running characteristics, several of their features which were not usually employed in British locomotive practice had given trouble. To overcome these difficulties, modifications were being carried out on the whole class and the locomotive tested was the second to be dealt with.

Controlled Road Tests were made between Salisbury and Exeter in both directions on special trains running to fairly fast schedules, but fitting in with normal services. The highest rate of working was 32,000lb of steam per hour with a coal rate of 4,780lb/hr, the limitation being imposed by the capacity of the tender to provide for the minimum test and acceptable warming up periods.

To follow the Controlled Road Tests, it was arranged for the locomotive to work certain representative service trains between Waterloo and Exeter. The western section of this route was that over which the Controlled Road Tests had been made.

The 'Merchant Navy' class had long enjoyed a reputation for high performance under adverse conditions and it was hoped that some comparative evidence would be obtained during the trials, especially as the western section of the route was particularly conducive to high performance. As it fortunately happened, the accident of contingencies resulted in what must rank as among the best performances of the 'Merchant Navy' locomotives. Further, there were no mechanical troubles and the valve gear proved as flexible as any normal arrangement.

On all the tests the locomotive steamed freely, and on the Controlled Road Tests, amongst the hundreds of samples of smokebox gas taken, all were apparently free of carbon monoxide, which indeed could be produced only when access of air to the ashpan was intentionally restricted. Similarly, on the service trains it appeared temporarily only when the fireman was building up the firebed in anticipation of the driver requiring a high power output.

These tests effectively disposed of some gossip alleging the inferiority of the rebuilds and their inability to 'run'. Indeed S. O. Ell, responsible for testing at Swindon, commented to Townroe during one of the Exeter to Salisbury test runs that 'The rebuilt "Merchant Navy" is very nearly a match for our "King" class'; which, says Townroe to the Author, 'is the greatest compliment a Great Western man could bring himself to pay!'

After these outstandingly successful tests, the rebuilding of the Pacifics went rapidly ahead. The first 15 of the 'Merchant Navy' class were modified by May 1957 and the remainder by October 1959. The first of the 'West Country' class was completed in May 1957 and 15 were in service by August 1958. Owing to the approaching phase-out of steam, however, rebuilding of the 'West Countries' stopped in 1961, when 60 engines had been converted. The remaining 50 retained their original appearance until they were withdrawn from service.

Notes

1 Townroe, S. C.: information to the Author
Riddles, R. A.: information to the Author
2 Letter from CM&EE SR to Locomotive Works Manager Eastleigh, 25 March 1955
3 Memorandum of meeting
4 CM&EE Letter of 16 June 1955
5 CM&EE Letter dated 5 July 1955
6 CM&EE Letter dated 15 May 1956

These three shots show No 34102 *Bere Alston* being rebuilt in 1961, this was the final locomotive, being the sixtieth Light Pacific to be so treated.

Above: The engine in the process of being stripped, already the 'air-smoothed' casing over the firebox has been removed and the fitters are engaged in burning away the cab supports to allow removal of the cab. The entire engine has been lifted clear of the wheels, which are seen in the right foreground. Various fittings have been removed including the injectors under the cab. The extreme left shows a rebuilt engine under repair.

Left: The only major modification to the boiler was the substitution of the Bulleid type smokebox for the traditional circular type, note the unusual length of the same. The uniquely shaped smokebox door was however retained. The circular handle, seen to the right of the dome, is the manifold shut off valve, which fed steam to the cab fittings.

Left: The boiler being lowered on to the frames, the section of sheeting which has been removed shows the lagging, at the firebox end some of the cab fittings are in place including the driver's brake valve. Note the wash-out plugs and the recesses in the casing, the inclined one being for the reverser shaft. On the chassis the reverser bracket and gearing have been added.
All Crown Copyright, National Railway Museum

35018
BRITISH INDIA
LINE
MERCHANT
NAVY CLASS
35018

35004

Above left: The first of the 90 Bulleid Pacifics to be modified was 'Merchant Navy' No 35018 *British India Line,* most of the Pacifics received modified tenders during or before rebuilding commenced. *BR*

Left: The 13.00 Waterloo-Exeter climbs away from Templecombe on 4 November 1961 headed by No 35004 *Cunard White Star.* *G. A. Richardson*

Above: The down 'Bournemouth Belle' headed by No 35012 *United States Lines* passing Millbrook on 10 March 1963. *R. A. Panting*

Centre right: No 35013 *Blue Funnel Line,* working the 13.30 Waterloo-Weymouth, arrives at the new island platform at Micheldever on 18 March 1967, the 'new' platform is devoid of all facilities. *J. H. Bird*

Bottom right: No 35023 *Holland-Afrika Line* minus nameplates is turned at Nine Elms mpd on 3 June 1967, one month before withdrawal. *J. Scrace*

Top right: ***Holland-Afrika Line*** **stands at Paddington at the head of a Ian Allan special from Plymouth in September 1958.** *G. Hogg*

Centre right: No 35020 ***Bibby Line*** **in rebuilt condition fitted with an unrebuilt tender in May 1956.** *LPC*

Below: Ex-works at Eastleigh is No 35029 ***Ellerman Lines,*** **fitted with a rebuilt high sided tender off one of the original batch of engines.**
G. H. Wheeler

Far right, top: No 35010 ***Blue Star*** **at Salisbury with the 16.00 Waterloo-Plymouth on 28 August 1960.** *K. L. Cook*

Far right, bottom: No 35026 ***Lamport & Holt Line*** **at Stockport Edgeley mpd, the engine was up north to work a rail tour.** *J. R. Carter*

35010
24
835

35026

GOLDEN
ARROW

Left: No 35005 *Canadian Pacific* speeds along the edge of Salisbury Plain on the approach to Warminster with a Warwickshire Railway Society special from Waterloo to Eastleigh and Swindon, returning to Paddington on 23 May 1965.
Brian Stephenson

Below left: No 35015 *Rotterdam Lloyd* on the down 'Golden Arrow' at Sydenham Hill. *R.C.Riley*

Right: No 35010 *Blue Star* at Nine Elms mpd, the driver is oiling the locomotive prior to taking coal. *D. Hermon*

Below: No 35023 *Holland-Afrika Line,* ready for the next duty. *G. H. Marsh*

35028
35028
SPL
2

Above left: No 35028 *Clan Line* takes water at Southampton Central on the return from Bournemouth, on one of the last steam specials on the Southern Region in July 1967. *E. Knight*

Left: No 35030 *Elder-Dempster Line* minus plates, unusually taking water at Winchester with the 08.35 Waterloo-Weymouth express on 15 June 1967. *J. C. McIver*

Above: Rebuilt 'Merchant Navy' No 35024 *East Asiatic Company* awaits the right of way from Templecombe with a down train, as an up train enters the station behind unrebuilt 'West Country' No 34106 *Lydford*. *Paul Riley*

Right: No 35023 the erstwhile *Holland-Afrika Line* with the final down steam worked train from Waterloo to Weymouth in July 1967. *G. P. Cooper*

7
The modified Pacifics

Opinions have been expressed that the rebuilt Pacifics lacked the brilliance of their air-smoothed predecessors, and the views of some drivers have been cited in support. Nevertheless, it is difficult to find justification for them; certainly nobody could complain that the rebuilds were lacking in speed. Driver E. Rabbetts of Bournemouth, for instance, during the week before he retired, was timed past S. C. Townroe's Shawford garden at 102mile/h with a rebuilt 'Merchant Navy'. Reasons have already been given for the enginemen's liking for Bulleid's original design. Many people have gained their impressions from platform conversations with drivers awaiting the 'right away' or relaxing after arrival. Drivers are by nature conservative men and are often particularly critical about any newly-built locomotive or one recently introduced from elsewhere. The author has heard adverse comments on the 'LMS engines', in reference to the Riddles Standard locomotives for British Railways, and once at Waterloo he was told that the Great Western pannier tanks, recently acquired for empty carriage stock working, were 'not nearly as good as ours' (ie the Drummond LSWR 0-4-4 tank engines). And at Paddington the driver of a 'Castle', on being asked whether he was looking forward to the arrival of the diesels, replied, 'Not while we have engines like these.' Similarly, at Kings Cross, the driver of 'A4' Pacific *Silver Fox*, waiting to go out on a down express and who had come up on a 'Deltic', was pleased to be driving a real engine again.

However, whether or not the modified 'Merchant Navy' and 'West Country' class Pacifics performed as well as they did in their unrebuilt state is a rather academic question, because the rebuilds were infinitely superior in consistency of performance, even after high mileages, and their vastly reduced maintenance requirements were an inestimable boon at a time when the recruitment of running shed fitters was particularly difficult. Maintenance costs were of course reduced as well, and there were further savings in the much less time taken in disposal work — that is, work on shed in turning the engine, filling up with coal and water, emptying the smokebox and ashpan, and cleaning the fire. This saving was due primarily to rocking grates that really worked; so that a rebuilt engine could be disposed within an hour, as compared with the two hours required with an unmodified Pacific, owing to the lengthy business of cleaning fires with the clinker shovel through the firehole door. In short, the rebuilding had given the Southern a stud of modern express passenger locomotives that could bear comparison with any other in the country.

The first modified 'Merchant Navy' Pacific went to Nine Elms Motive Power Depot, which was chosen for the initial allocation because the depot mechanical staff were below strength and the modified engines were certain to afford some relief in the amount of routine attention needed.

Nine Elms had suffered badly during the air raids of 1940-41. Its tall coal-hopper, stripped by bomb blasts of its exterior cladding, stood like a gaunt skeleton; the roofs of the sheds and workshops, patched with corrugated asbestos, were not completely rain-proof; and though various schemes for rebuilding were prepared, they were postponed from year to year. Its condition was criticised severely when the main line diesel locomotives had to be serviced there while working on the Western Section during 1953-54. The condition of the depot was so bad, indeed, that there was a proposal to build a modern replacement at Clapham Junction which would have had separate sections for steam and diesel, and would have been more convenient for the train-berthing sidings there. However, the scheme came to nothing and Nine Elms deteriorated steadily until its ultimate closure. This was the state of affairs when the first modified Pacifics arrived and it is not surprising that many vacancies for mechanics remained unfilled. The two other big London Depots, Bricklayers Arms and Stewarts Lane, had been helping by taking in some of the Nine Elms ailing unmodified Pacifics; not that their condition was much superior but they were better equipped with workshops.

The mechanical shortcomings of the unmodified Pacifics would not have resulted in so many days and weeks out of service if the Southern sheds had been provided with machine tools, lifting hoists, and drop pits on the scale of the concentration depots on other Regions. The Great Western sheds were almost lavishly equipped and were the envy of Southern men. But it had been the policy on the Southern Railway to have casual repairs of all kind dealt with at Eastleigh and Ashford Works, rather than to equip the sheds. This system, however, catered very well for the solid, reliable locomotives designed by Maunsell and Urie, and it had the advantage that the capital value of locomotive spares held at the motive power depots could be kept to a minimum. The Works, on the other hand, had the specialists, the machines, and a comprehensive stock of spares to deal with every contingency.

The unmodified Pacifics did not fit into this system at all. The proportion of spares held at depots for them had to be increased considerably; but the greater problem was that of transporting to and from Works the unprecedented number of motion parts that needed reconditioning in the Works after mileages of from 30,000 to 36,000. Large parts such as wheels, would travel by wagon and take time. Small parts were, by long custom, put on tenders, suitably wrapped and labelled, and would normally be delivered within 24 hours. By the early 1950s the amount of material in transit to keep the Pacifics running was overloading the system. At Ashford mpd and Eastleigh mpd, unloading and loading parts in transit between the adjacent Works and the various other mpds needed extra staff to handle it. Furthermore, the backs of tenders were not the best places to carry such items as coupling rods, and soon with natural reluctance, road transport had to be used despite the extra expense.

The opinion of Shedmasters, who had to look after the unmodified Pacifics, was expressed by John Pringle, formerly in charge of Bournemouth Central mpd, who wrote:

'You dare not risk letting them exceed the 36,000-mile front-end and motion exams. These could stop an engine for a fortnight or more and we could not afford to do so during the summer train service, when our Pacifics would run their mileage in a few months. I had to get all the engines examined, whether due or not, before the end of May. Likewise, any with high mileages would be booked for Eastleigh Works well in advance. The rebuilds were a great relief; exams only due at 44-48,000 miles and you could safely let them go a bit longer, if need be. And you would probably only need to do the exams once between the Works Intermediate repairs; with the unmodified engines we would have to do them three times before "shopping"!'

Of the unmodified Pacifics he added: 'We got so used to bent coupling rods that we would straighten them by putting a screw jack against the shed wall! Officially we were expected to take the rods off and send them to Eastleigh, but that took too long. It didn't seem to do any harm; we never had a broken coupling rod.'

The rebuilds consumed noticeably less coal and water. The high consumption of the originals caused coaling difficulties at the motive power depots. Although the tenders held five tons, it was almost standard practice for engines to take more coal immediately before leaving a depot. Nearly a ton would be burnt in building up the fire before departure and unless the engine had the coal stacked 'to the brim' there might not be sufficient to cover both outward and return journeys. Engines working the 'Bournemouth Belle', for instance, from Waterloo to Bournemouth West, and then going on to Branksome to turn, would frequently have to make a light trip to Bournemouth Central for more coal in order to get the 'Belle' safely back to Waterloo. More than one unmodified Pacific was completely out of coal when it drew up at the platform at Waterloo and had to be towed home to Nine Elms. One unlucky driver, his engine very low in steam, was stopped by signal outside Waterloo and was unable to re-start. Assistance was needed and the train eventually stopped at the arrival platform half-an-hour late. The delay incensed one of the passengers, the wife of a senior member of British Railways, and the following day her husband demanded a special report. Waterloo's special report was brief — 'Dusty coal'. This was if anything an understatement for dust was about all that was left.

Driver Peter Smith, in his book *Mendip Enginemen*,[1] describes how, in order to work an unmodified 'West Country' engine from Bath to Bournemouth West and back over the 143 miles of the difficult Somerset & Dorset line, the best part of a tub of coal would be stacked on the footplate and the tender then topped up to the maximum it would hold with safety. One day, indeed, the tender was so full that the shedmaster insisted on passing it under a loading gauge for fear that it would not get through the tunnels.

The shortcomings of the original 'West Country' Pacifics were particularly revealed on the Somerset & Dorset line. Their uncertain adhesion on the gradients cut down their class rating from 7 to 5 and the LMS Class 5 4-6-0s proved able to perform just as well and burnt less coal. When the new Riddles BR Class 5 4-6-0s were delivered to Nine Elms and Stewarts Lane in the mid-1950s, drivers gladly took one to cover an unmodified 'West Country' duty, because the harder it worked, the more it seemed able to take. At Nine Elms there were times when, owing to stoppages of Pacifics, a BR '5' was put on the 'Bournemouth Belle'. It was a revelation to the Nine Elms men to find that the engine kept time and that the firemen actually did not have to use his shovel as much.

It is with the foregoing in mind that the modified Pacifics should be judged, and not by comparing their performances with those of the originals. Anyway, tests and trials made with the unmodified and modified versions by observers from outside the Southern Region proved that, whilst the original Pacifics were capable of some outstanding performances, they were unpredictable and temperamental; and that the rebuilt engines were not only reliable but their achievements were in no way inferior to those of their unrebuilt precursors. There was no foundation for any opinions to the contrary expressed by drivers.

In fact, the rebuilt engines included many improvements for drivers and firemen. The look-out in both directions was improved; thanks to a fully-wrapped boiler, the cabs were not so oppressively hot in summer; the sanding gear worked properly and any slipping was controlled by the improved regulator; the water gauges could be read more easily by both enginemen without having to leave their seats and a burst gauge glass could be isolated at the drop of a handle; the cut-off setting was locked and could not creep; there were no sump oil pressure gauges to worry about; the clear-reading tender water gauges provided a sure indication of how much remained to take the engine to the next water column, so that hasty topping up for safety at intermediate stopping stations was not needed; and, finally, if the stiffer coupled wheel springs made the riding rather less easy, they were less responsive to soft places in the permanent way and so reduced any tendency for the engine to roll. These various alterations from former practice put the driver much more at ease during the journey.[2]

In connection with sanding, there is a faintly amusing postscript to the use of sanding on tenders (intended for tender-first working). On 9 November 1962 the Works Manager at Eastleigh issued the following instruction: 'With reference . . . to the condition of the tender sandboxes on the unmodified "West Country" class locomotives, will you please note that when they have been removed for repairs they need not be replaced. For the time being will you please retain the equipment in case an appeal is made by the Motive Power Dept for sanding gear to be refitted . . ' He then sent a report to the CM&EE (confirming a telephone conversation) stating that, 'due to the condition of the tender sandboxes caused by the ingress of water and the rusty state of the control gear' the equipment served little purpose and he was arranging to remove it as engines passed through the Works for heavy repair. The CM&EE replied that he agreed, and someone made a pencilled comment on his letter: 'Just as well! Many done.'

The troubles that beset the modified engines were comparatively minor, and of these the most interesting were the ejection of live coal, causing lineside fires; inaccurate valve setting, causing knocks; frame fractures at the trailing end of the 'West Country' class; and cracking and bulging of the thermic syphons.

The problem presented by the ejection of live coal from the chimney was submitted in January 1961 to the CME, British Transport Commission. It was dealt with by the BR Locomotive Testing Committee, who forwarded it to the Swindon Testing Plant for report. This elicited, on 13 February 1961, a paper with the mammoth title of a *Memorandum on Possible Modifications to the Le Maitre* (sic) *Type Ejector on S.R. Locomotives to Eliminate Harmful Live-Coal Ejections and Improve Steaming and Smoke Ejection.* After ejecting this lot, one feels that the author must have paused for replenishment!

The report, in fact, gives an interesting account of the theory of locomotive exhaust and the measures that have been taken to improve its efficiency; though rather strangely it does not mention the Kylchap exhaust which practical experience on the LNER and the SNCF had shown to be the most efficient of all.

In 1891 Professor W. F. M. Goss undertook scientific experiments into locomotive exhaust, and the results appeared in his book *Locomotive Performance*, which had considerable influence on British engineers. The object sought in an efficient exhaust is to mix the exhaust steam and the gases from the fire so thoroughly that the whole is expelled from the chimney with the minimum of effort, as already stated in Chapter 2. Goss showed the highly important action in the chimney whereby the velocity of the flue gases induced to flow upwards in the space between blastpipe and chimney rises as they ascend whilst the velocity of the steam jet falls. The entraining action is complete when the peripheral velocities of steam and gas are equal. The core of the steam jet, however, remains at a much higher velocity than the peripheral steam, and, whilst it sustains velocity in the latter, a high proportion of its energy remains unused. This entraining, or mixing, needs room to develop, but it did not present a problem when Goss wrote because the smokeboxes of most locomotives were small and their chimneys consequently long. W. F. Pettigrew, who was intimately concerned with the design and construction of W. Adams' express passenger 4-4-0s for the LSWR, wrote that chimneys were generally conical, slightly smaller in diameter at the bottom than the top. The inside diameter of the chimney was of the greatest importance and it was usually made about two inches less than that of the cylinders.[3]

As boilers, and therefore smokeboxes, grew larger, chimneys became shorter and proportions became critical because of restricted room. Bulleid had got hold of Goss's book in 1904, and from it he set out the appropriate chimney and petticoat shape to suit Ivatt's large Great Northern Atlantics, but found to his surprise that it hardly differed from Ivatt's own design. Bulleid asked how the design had been worked out and was told that the Drawing Office had produced a proposal based on previous practice and Ivatt had this drawn at full size. He then made a number of alterations to the sweep of the petticoat and the chimney taper and outline.[4] It is hardly surprising, therefore, that a GN Atlantic, fitted with a shorter chimney to suit the LNER loading gauge, did not do as well as expected on trials in comparison with NB and NE Atlantics.

To investigate the best proportions in an era of large boilers, many controlled experiments were conducted at the Swindon Testing Plant on empirically proportioned chimneys which were known to be successful in practice. From these experiments the best proportions were deduced to enable a short chimney to function as efficiently as a long one. Nevertheless, the minimum height of such a chimney was too short for many large locomotives, and the loading gauge prevented it from being lengthened. The extra length could, however, be provided by having a double chimney and double blastpipe; thereby increasing also the chimney and blastpipe diameters. This arrangement entails a drop in the initial velocity given to the gases, but there is also a reduction in the peak values of smokebox vacuum, which are mainly responsible for lifting the larger ash and coals from the firebed.

The matter can be pursued further from these two blastpipes, or jets, in line to say seven of them. This would be unacceptably long, but the length at base could be reduced and the arrangement made acceptable by fanning out the jets from base to atmosphere and making the seven chimneys, or entraining tubes, of rectangular instead of circular section. This would be essentially the same as the Giesl ejector, which shows that the latter embodies no new principle.

Experience with a Giesl, on a boiler roughly comparable with that of the 'West Country' locomotives, was provided by one fitted to a BR Standard 2-10-0 working heavy coal trains in South Wales. With this the lift from the fire was confined to particles even smaller than those ejected from an engine having a normal self-cleaning arrangement.

Tests of the Giesl at Rugby showed an increase in indicated horsepower of from 4.8 to 7.25% and a saving in coal of 3.72% at average rates of working. However, the higher savings claimed for the Giesl were not realised, nor would the device enable a locomotive to burn unsuitable coal, as had also been claimed. This result was not surprising because the Giesl ejector only provides air for combustion and cannot have much other influence on the combustion process. The tests did however encourage the view that a properly designed multi-jet arrangement would be a solution to the Southern Region's problem.

As the retention of as much as possible of the existing Lemaître system was desirable, the adaptation of its multi-jet ejector had been examined, and a modification was proposed which would probably be just as efficient as the Giesl exhaust. A reduction in the outlet area compared with that of the existing chimney should provide a better 'lift' of the exhaust, and a considerable reduction in the pre-chimney action and chimney access should render spark arrestors unnecessary. It was estimated that the five jets could be opened up to provide a total jet area of 30sq in, and that the consequent saving of coal and water should be significant.

No action, in fact, was taken on the report, and it is probable that, owing to the approaching demise of steam, the suggested modification for such a comparatively slight benefit was not considered worthwhile. Indeed, unless the exhaust of a locomotive needs improvement to enable it to do the job for which it was designed, it is probably best left alone; and, as Colonel K. R. N. Cameron, one time Motive Power Superintendent, Scotland, wrote in a letter to the Author: 'There has probably been more steam blown off in the metaphorical sense than ever passed through the blastpipes themselves!'

Townroe, in fact, rather questions the apparent assumption that the modified Pacifics were more likely to cause lineside fires than any other type. It was seldom possible, he says, to identify any particular train as the cause of a fire; for by the time the outbreak had been discovered a number of trains would have passed the site, and any one of them could have been responsible. The New Forest was in his District and the Forestry Commission sensibly left the lineside clear, so that there were no claims. It was the farming area between Winchester and Basingstoke that was the source of occasional claims in a dry summer. The Legal Department of the railway would send the claim forms to be filled in, but it was quite impossible to prepare accurate statements. The culprit would therefore be arbitrarily selected as, say, the engine of the 2.30pm Weymouth to Waterloo, which in 1960 could well have been a modified Pacific!

When Townroe saw the depth of the smokebox, from front to back, on the first modified Pacific, he thought there might be difficulty in emptying the ash without a special long-handled shovel; but observations of disposal work at Nine Elms proved that most of the 'char' piled up against the smokebox door, and very little lay beyond the normal reach of an ordinary fireman's shovel. There was a huge capacity for the char to collect undisturbed, and it seemed likely to diminish spark-throwing. There was plenty of room for spark arresting screens if necessary. The British Railways standard arrangement could have been used, but presumably fire claims were not sufficiently costly to justify fitting it.

The Locomotive Testing Committee, who directed the investigation, was one of the British Railways Technical Committees which met regularly at Marylebone, and was responsible, amongst other matters, for the work done on the Swindon Testing Plant.

The first modified 'Merchant Navy' locomotives, after running between 30,000 and 40,000 miles, developed a knock and by August 1957 investigations into this phenomenon were being carried out on engine No 35025 *Brocklebank Line*.[5] These took the form of tests on the Stationary Testing Plant at Swindon and showed that the pressures attained at the front end of the cylinders exceeded those at the back end by from 60 to 100psi under normal conditions of working with full regulator. It was considered that this difference arose from the relative expansions of the valve spindles and frames because, as the valves were set when the engines were cold, the setting was likely to be upset when running at normal temperatures. The valves of No 35025 were therefore altered; those of the middle cylinder (with inside admission) being moved back $^1/_{16}$in, and those of the outside cylinders (with outside admission) being moved forward $^1/_{16}$in. This adjustment was successful in equalising the peak pressures, and subsequent running in the Testing Plant showed that the knock had been eliminated. Instructions were accordingly issued to the Locomotive Works Manager, Eastleigh, that in future the valves of the modified Pacifics of both classes were to be set when cold so that the valve heads of the outside cylinders were $^1/_{16}$in ahead of the correct drawing position and those of the middle cylinder $^1/_{16}$in behind it. An interesting addition was that there had been similar experiences with LMR and BR engines, so that on these the valve heads should be set $^1/_{16}$in behind the correct drawing position when cold.

The CM&EE wrote on 18 September 1957 to the Motive Power Superintendent at Waterloo in answer to an enquiry from him on this matter. He said that without the modification considerable compression was occurring at the front ends of each cylinder; a condition that probably caused a greater disturbance at high speed, when a locomotive was working at a short cut-off. Severe loading was then applied to the boxes, which could cause longitudinal wear in the journal bearings. Such wear would eventually cause knocking, and the axleboxes when that happened would have to be reconditioned. This had been done in respect of No 35026 which was now running very smoothly indeed.

On 15 February 1960 the CM&EE wrote to the Locomotive Works Manager, Eastleigh, referring to complaints about the valve setting on No 35010 when it was released from Works in July 1959 after Intermediate repairs. Trials carried out at the time showed that the locomotive was capable of dealing with all normal rostered duties, and it was decided to take action only if there was a deterioration in performance. Such deterioration had now occurred, and to such an extent that drivers were having considerable difficulty in starting trains of 400 tons and over. In any case the engine would have to be withdrawn from service owing to the condition of the eccentric strap and inside big end bearing.

In spite of the above episode, it appears that the critical setting of the valve gears gradually escaped attention and time-keeping was affected. The CM&EE's Department accordingly wrote to the Works Manager Eastleigh on 23 September 1963 saying that a previous Works Manager had laid it down that checking of valve events should be confined to General repairs, and it had immediately been pointed out to him that General repairs were only carried out at intervals of about 300,000 miles, during which time valve gears details would have been overhauled twice, if not three times, at Intermediate repairs, so that settings could fall far below an efficient standard. It had been suggested, therefore, that valve events should be checked at each Intermediate repair, and it was apparent that compliance with this suggestion had lapsed.

This case history is of interest in showing how a slight departure from the critical valve setting could cause knock (and consequent wear in journal bearings) and so mar locomotive performance as to affect time-keeping.

In 1962 some concern was expressed at the incidence of frame fractures among the 'West Country' class Pacifics, both modified and unmodified. A total of 60 engines had been modified and the remaining 50 remained unmodified. The trouble was brought to light after unmodified No 34033, *Chard*, was released to traffic following a General repair, and was found after inspection at Bournemouth Motive Power Depot to have a fractured frame behind the left trailing horn. Previously, on 14 December 1961, an unmodified engine, No 34067 *Tangmere*, had been accepted for Intermediate repair, and examination of the main frames disclosed a fracture behind the right trailing horn which had not been reported by the Salisbury Motive Power Depot. As a result of these failures a survey was made of the Frame Record Cards of the other 'West Country' class engines, and it was found that 14 of the modified and 27 of the unmodified had had fractured trailing end frames repaired by welding. Of the modified engines, three had had two fractures and one three. The record of the unmodified engines was worse, for eight had had two fractures, six had had three, two had had four, and one had had five. Cracks in the frames were, incidentally, difficult to see in the Sheds because they were hidden behind the BFB wheels. This state of affairs was the subject of a report issued by the Locomotive Works Manager, Eastleigh, on 7 March 1962. He was concerned at the method of repair used which he considered had been only partially successful and he attached a sketch showing a suggested improvement.

The matter was not, in fact, as serious as it would appear because there is no indication that there was a risk of completely broken frames. The 110 'West Countries' were from 11 to 17 years old, had run a considerable mileage, and each of them had from four to six General repairs. The Works internal correspondence reveals, however, that the Erecting Shop had been making quick repairs of the cracks in the interest of output. The result was bad workmanship and inadequate supervision. The particular interest of the report is that it brings to light the increased vigilance that is necessary in maintaining an ageing fleet of locomotives.[6]

The problems with the thermic syphons in both classes of Pacific were caused by the build-up of scale deposits inside them and the development of transverse cracks. The Works Metallurgist at Eastleigh had reported in 1962 that he considered the period at which repairs were deemed necessary varied between 9 and 16 years. However, by 1965 a number of locomotives were being stopped for syphon repair after far less than nine years in service. New syphon plates fitted to 'West Country' locomotives Nos 34032 and 34059 at their last General repairs in October and March 1960 respectively were showing signs of cracking. Build-up of scale deposits had been found in the thermic syphons of No 34008 and 34064, and a syphon of the former had started to bulge. As regards the cracks, it was confirmed that the correct type of plate had been used in manufacture and it was suggested that overheating might have been a contributory factor in transverse cracks developing so rapidly. An investigation was to be carried out to ascertain if footplate staff were using the correct firing techniques. To prevent the build-up of scale a procedure was laid down which was to be followed at the boiler washout.[7]

The remark about correct firing techniques is puzzling; for it is not clear how a method of firing could affect the thermic syphons, and the water-treatment gear should have prevented scaling. S. C. Townroe believes that the troubles with the syphons were isolated cases, and, as both modified and unmodified Pacifics had their original boilers, it may have been a symptom of age. Certainly there was no serious trouble in the Running Sheds over the thermic syphons, and Townroe never heard of failures on the road caused by leaking cracks, nor of even minor disasters from weld failures.

The advisability of fitting thermic syphons at all has been disputed. When R. A. Riddles was in America, Stanier asked him to find out from Emerson, Chief of Motive Power on the Delaware & Hudson Railroad, what his opinion was of thermic syphons. The latter told him of the many maintenance troubles they had had with them, and Riddles feels that this may well have been the reason why Stanier never even considered them for the engines he designed for British Railways[8]

Having discussed the minor troubles that beset these excellent rebuilt locomotives, it will be appreciated how very minor indeed they were compared with the sea of troubles that inundated the original design.

Notes

1 Smith, Driver Peter; *Mendip Enginemen;* Oxford Publishing Company, 1972
2 For most of the chapter up to this point I am indebted to S. C. Townroe
3 Pettigrew, W. F.; *A Manual of Locomotive Engineering*; London, Charles Griffin & Co, 2nd Edn 1901, p227
4 Bulleid, H. A. V.; *Master Builders of Steam*; London, Ian Allan Ltd, 1963, p72
5 CM&EE letter to Locomotive Works Manager Eastleigh, 19 August 1957
6 Eastleigh Works Internal Correspondence 1962
7 Eastleigh Works Internal Correspondence 1965
8 Riddles, R. A.; information to the Author

Below left: An up Continental is headed by No 34005 *Barnstaple* at Sydenham Hill; this engine was the first of 60 Light Pacifics to be rebuilt. *R. C. Riley*

Right: The driver of rebuilt 'West Country' No 34013 *Okehampton* chats to the signalman at Seaton Junction while working the 09.50 (SO) Portsmouth-Plymouth on 5 September 1964. *Paul Riley*

Below: No 34039 *Boscastle* seen in January 1959, paired with a new 5,250gal tender body attached to the original underframe. *C. P. Boocock*

WAITING
LIMITED
TO 60 MINS
IN ANY
2HOURS
WPH
2

Left: No 34021 *Dartmoor* passes Horley on the up local line with the Saturday Eastbourne–Manchester train on 25 July 1964. *G. D. King*

Below left: The 'Pines Express' relief is headed by No 34045 *Ottery St Mary* seen here waiting for a pilot at Evercreech Junction in August 1961. *G. W. Morrison*

Above right: No 34058 *Sir Frederick Pile* enters Bere Alston with a train from Plymouth, on 9 September 1962. The Callington branch is on the right of the picture. *L. Nicholson*

Right: 34096 *Trevone* on the 17.00 Waterloo-Yeovil Town leaving Milborne Port Halt on May 18 1964. *M. Mensing*

Below: No 34060 *25 Squadron* leaves Weymouth with a train for Waterloo on 13 August 1966, banked by another Light Pacific. *D. E.Canning*

34016

Above left: Storming out of Pophams Tunnel at Micheldever is No 34047 *Callington* with the 11.07 Bournemouth-Waterloo train on 20 March 1967. *IAL*

Left: The up 'Bournemouth Belle' is seen here climbing Beaulieu Road bank in the New Forest headed by No 34026 *Yes Tor* on 16 August 1960. *J. H. Bird*

Below left: No 34016 *Bodmin* on the 08.35 Bournemouth West-Waterloo near Winchester on 12 October 1962. This is one of several rebuilt Light Pacifics that have been preserved. *L. Elsey*

Above: The 17.09 Basingstoke commuter train leaves Woking behind No 34013 on 6 June 1967. *G. D. King*

Right: No 34052 *Lord Dowding* on a Bournemouth train hurrying it through Deepcut on 30 April 1966. *G. P. Cooper*

Left: No 34100 *Appledore* stands at Shepperton on 5 February 1967 with the 'South Western Suburban' rail tour. *E. Knight*

Centre left: No 34004 *Yeovil* on Sole Street bank with a Ramsgate-Victoria express in May 1959. *P. Ransome-Wallis*

Bottom left: No 34012 *Launceston* works the 09.10 Charing Cross to Dover and Ramsgate into Waterloo (Eastern) on 25 October 1960. *J. Scrace*

Below: No 34100 leaving Windsor & Eton Riverside with the 'South Western Suburban' rail tour on 5 February 1967. *M. Pope*

LCGB
TOUR
100
100
1953 1967
SOUTH WESTERN
SUBURBAN
RAIL TOUR

34088
6

113
85

Above left: Running over the Catford loop, No 34088 *145 Squadron* on the 16.10 Victoria–Folkestone Harbour at Catford on 28 May 1961.
J. Scrace

Left: A down Ashford train containing TPOs between Paddock Wood and Morden on 3 August 1959 hauled by No 34027 *Taw Valley*.
G. M. Kichenside

Above: No 34089 *602 Squadron* slips heavily at Waterloo while attempting to start its Weymouth bound expres. *M. J. Esau*

Right: No 34090 *Sir Eustace Missenden Southern Railway* races downhill into Buckhorn Weston Tunnel near Templecombe with the 08.35 (SO) Waterloo–Exeter on 7 September 1963.
G. A. Richardson

8
Summary

On looking back over the history of Bulleid's Pacifics, one is faced with two questions; firstly, why were such expensive and troublesome locomotives tolerated for so long before being rebuilt into the excellent engines that they eventually became, and secondly, were they, in any case, the right type of engines to meet the Southern's traffic needs at the time they were introduced?

The answer to the first question must take into account the situation on the Southern Railway and its successor, the Southern Region, during the early period of British Railways. The last 10 of the 'Merchant Navy' class, completed in 1948-49, were started before the Southern Railway ceased to exist; the building of the Light Pacifics started in 1945 and went well on into BR days — the last of them being completed in 1951. Thus the first of the 'West Country' class emerged four years after some defects in the design had become evident, and production went on steadily to a total of 110 over the next six years! It is difficult to think of a similar episode in railway history.

After the war was over the organisation of the Southern Railway was adjusted gradually to the peacetime conditions. Senior officers who had been retained during the war beyond the age of retirement were replaced, and departments evacuated from London were uprooted from their bucolic environment to return to their old offices, or to somewhere in the vicinity. The management was too busy coping with day-to-day routine, and in getting train services back to normal, to question the wisdom of its CME. Nationalisation was obviously imminent so that decisions affecting the future were rather naturally deferred. Nationalisation, indeed, had an early influence on Southern locomotive affairs, for, in imitation of the LMS motive power organisation, the new Locomotive Running Superintendent appointed in 1945 was no longer a Chief Officer but came under the Traffic Manager. This was an unhappy arrangement because it placed the Locomotive Running Department within a non-technical branch which had no knowledge of locomotive engineering and no interest in it so long as the trains ran to time.

It was during 1946-48 that Bulleid managed to persuade the Traffic authorities that the modern branch line tank locomotives, for which they had asked, should take the form of 0-6-6-0s, to be known as the 'Leader' class. Consent was given for five to be constructed, despite the absence of any precise specification. It was only when the first 'Leader' took shape, with the same unreliable valve gear as the Pacifics together with many other novelties of speculative reliability, that warning voices were heard from the Locomotive Running people; and on their advice a submission for a total of 35 'Leaders' was held up pending trial running. As things turned out, it was just as well!

The first 'Leader' underwent abortive trials in June 1949. On the following 30 September Bulleid retired from British Railways and joined the Irish Railways (CIE). In November R. A. Riddles ordered work to be stopped on the remaining four engines, and in March 1951 the project was officially scrapped. Though the 'Leader' story has no direct connection with the Pacifics, it is conceivable that the credulous interest with which the idea was received by the Traffic Department, tended to divert attention from the problem of the Pacifics; particularly as, from a purely traffic point of view, there were so many of them that the number out of service did not result in train cancellations.

When the new British Railways organisation was set up the Chief of Motive Power at Board level was given authority over the Regional Motive Power officers. The BR Chief of Motive Power, Colonel Harold Rudgard, ex-Midland and ex-LMS, changed everything to LMS practices, bringing a big increase in paperwork for the Motive Power Depots. He was something of a martinet, and a very small man, who, says R. A. Riddles, always wore a bowler hat to make himself appear taller.[1] He was a practical engineer who toured round the mpds and soon heard about the maintenance difficulties. He would have supported any proposal to rebuild the Bulleid Pacifics, but Bulleid remained as Mechanical Engineer of the Southern Region until 1949, and whilst he was still in office courtesy would have prohibited active steps to that end. Bulleid had, in fact, allowed his technical and workshops staff to incorporate a large number of such modifications as could be carried out during overhauls, and which could be charged to the Engine Repair Account. It was apparent by 1950 that these were only palliatives which could not remedy the fundamental errors of the original design; but BR's designers were too engaged with the new Standard locomotives to consider tinkering with existing ones.

Under the new BR organisation, locomotives belonging to the different Regions were soon subjected to statistical assessment. One important Motive Power statistic was the percentage of locomotives in, or available, for service. The large fleet of modern Standard types built for the LMS returned a figure of 85% availability. This was well above that achieved on the Southern, and closer scrutiny revealed the extent to which the Regional average was adversely affected by the poor availability of the 140 Bulleid Pacifics. By 1947 it had become necessary for all Depots with Pacifics to report daily to Headquarters at 7am, stating, in respect of each locomotive, whether it was in service and, if not, the reason for its stoppage. This special reporting system was essential because a back-log of Pacific repairs at one depot could only be relieved by having their repairs carried out at another depot. The annual mileage of the Pacifics averaged only about 50,000, and their availability very rarely exceeded 65%. Their high coal consumption, as compared with equivalent locomotives of other Regions, had been shown in the Interchange Trials of 1948.[2]

The loan of some of the 'West Country' class to Stratford mpd for work on the East Anglian lines was an eye-opener for those who had not realised the maintenance problems with which the Southern men had to contend; for the very competent Stratford fitters were confronted with troubles they had never encountered before. Their comments on the 'spam-cans' were lurid and there were no further requests for the loan of these engines by the Eastern or any other Region: the word had got round!

The above, then, were the various factors that combined to keep the Pacifics at work in their original form, long after it was apparent that rebuilding would be economically justified. As has already been said, it is a tribute to the designer that the rebuilt engines, which retained the major part of Bulleid's creation, were equal to any other express engines on British Railways.

The second question, that is, whether the Bulleid Pacifics were the engines needed at the time of their introduction and, if not, what should have been built, has been the subject of much discussion amongst Southern locomotive running men.[3]

Traffic on the Southern Railway was quite different from that on the other three great railway companies. On the LMS and LNER, particularly the reduction of say 10 minutes in travelling time was an attraction to business men in the Midlands and north-east, intending a journey to London and back during the day; but it was of minor importance to passengers travelling on the boat trains to the Kentish ports, or to those proceeding on their holidays to the Channel and Atlantic coast resorts. Business men on the Southern lived mostly in the London commuter belt, and the frequent and reasonably fast electric services met their needs. Minor time savings were not, therefore, worth the cost entailed.

Maunsell had left the Southern with a stock of good, reliable, and solidly built locomotives. The 'Nelsons' were fine engines, particularly as improved by Bulleid, but there were too few of them. The design was as recent as that of any express engine running on the Great Western up to the last days of steam. (The 'Kings' and 'Castles' were only enlargements of Churchward's 'Stars'.) More of them could have been built to cover the heaviest express services. The 'Arthurs' were good, though ageing, but the three-cylinder 4-4-0 'Schools' could do as well, if not better, on the less heavy express trains. A three-cylinder 4-6-0 version of the 'Schools' class would have been popular, and with up-to-date welding technique and a reduction in the amount of metal in splashers and running boards (as Riddles was to effect in his Standard engines), axle weights could have been kept within the Civil Engineer's limit for the lines west of Exeter and other secondary lines.

It is true that these 4-6-0s would not have been mixed traffic engines but as we have seen the Bulleid Pacifics were not suitable for freight work. The Southern already had the admirable 'S15' 4-6-0s for fast freight trains, but it was the only company without an eight-coupled freight engine. One must remember that the first Bulleid Pacifics were being constructed at the start of a major war, when passenger trains had a low priority and suffered a drastic reduction in speed. Running men would have preferred a 2-8-0 to either a mixed traffic locomotive or Bulleid's horrible looking 'Q1' class 0-6-0, which had insufficient brake power to work a heavy loose-coupled freight train. Southern men were delighted with the Riddles 'Austerity' 2-8-0s, which they had for all too short a time. A total of say 60 2-8-0s, using as much as possible of Maunsell standard motion parts and fittings, would have been of far greater value to the Southern than the 40 Pacifics which had been completed during the War.

The year 1946 would have been the right time to produce a new passenger locomotive. If it has been designed as the modified 'West Country' it would have been a great success. It could have run the heaviest and fastest trains just as well as a 'Merchant Navy', as was often demonstrated, with the advantage of wider route-availability. At that time a modern 2-6-2 tank engine could have replaced the antiquated and non-superheated branch line engines with greater economy in fuel consumption and repair costs. As it was, the Southern had to wait some eight years for the BR Class 2 tank.

This book represents an effort to record the facts, both the good and not so good, of a most interesting venture in steam locomotive design. If the troubles seem unduly prominent, criticism must be tempered by bearing in mind the circumstances of Bulleid's selection for his post. He was appointed Chief Mechanical Engineer by a Southern Railway Board of Directors who had a reputation for new ventures, and who had made the Southern a thoroughly go-ahead concern in all its many fields: electrification, signalling, docks and shipping, and smart operation of its trains. Bulleid was encouraged, therefore, in his attempts to reflect this new Southern image in his steam engines. George Stephenson, after all, did the same thing with the 'Rocket' — and that had to be modified too!

Notes

1 Riddles, R. A.: statement to the Author
2 Townroe, S. C.: information to the Author
3 *ibid*

Above: No 34100 *Appledore* departs from Victoria with the last steam hauled 'Golden Arrow' boat train for Dover Marine on 11 June 1961.
Brian Stephenson

Right: No 34089 *602 Squadron* at Stewarts Lane mpd in May 1963 near the end of steam operations at this shed. *J. Scrace*

Below right: No 34059 *Sir Archibald Sinclair* approaches Buckhorn Weston tunnel on 14 October 1961 with a freight from Salisbury.
G. A. Richarson

Above: Sunlight and shadows at Nine Elms mpd, No 34059 *Sir Archibald Sinclair* is undergoing examination. *P. Leavens*

Left: The down Waterloo-Salisbury express approaching Tunnel junction behind No 34050 *Royal Observer Corps*. *W. P. Conolly*

Below left: No 34025, the erstwhile *Whimple* waits for departure time at Waterloo, she lasted until the end of Southern steam. *IAL*

34024
394

Above left: The 17.41 ex-Salisbury rolls into Waterloo behind No 34026 *Yes Tor. Yes Tor* was withdrawn in September 1966.
D. MacKinnon

Left: No 34024, ex-*Tamar Valley* approaches Southampton Central with a Bournemouth-York train on 2 January 1967. *L. A. Nixon*

Above: No 34004 *Yeovil* waits her turn at the coaling stage at Nine Elms depot, the photo was taken on 24 September 1966. *I. M. McIvor*

Right: No 34087, formerly *145 Squadron* is in a clean condition considering that the end of steam is near, she is seen at Nine Elms in the early summer of 1967. *J. Wellard*

Below right: Rebuilt Pacifics No 34012 and 34052 stand silent at Nine Elms along with an unrebuilt engine. Their services dispensed with.
Eric Treacy

Appendices
1
The 1948 Locomotive Exchanges

In 1948 the newly-formed Railway Executive decided to institute a series of trials between locomotives of the four Regions. The trials were to be held between express, mixed traffic and freight engines. The locomotives that the Southern authorities chose were the 'Merchant Navy' and 'West Country' for the express and mixed traffic trials respectively.

The engines chosen were Nos 35017 *Belgian Marine,* 35019 *French Line C.G.T.* and 35020 *Bibby Line* representing the 'Merchant Navies' and Nos 34004 *Yeovil,* 34005 *Barnstaple* and 34006 *Bude* for the 'West Country' engines. All were prepared and fitted with LMR tenders with water pick-up facilities, No 34004 also had tablet changing apparatus fitted for working between Perth and Inverness. No 35020 did not, however, participate while No 35018 *British India Line* was the engine chosen for trials over Southern metals.

There is no need to record the performance here as the story of the trials are well documented elsewhere.

Above left: No 35017 *Belgian Marine* with an up train south of Kenton on 14 May 1948.
Wethersett Collection /IAL

Left: No 35017 *Belgian Marine* passes Holloway with the 13.10 Kings Cross-Leeds on 27 May 1948.
E. R. Wethersett/IAL

Above: No 35019 *French Line C.G.T.* attracts attention from the platform end as it departs from Paddington. *LPC*

Right: No 35019 *French Line C.G.T.* leaves Greenwood tunnel on the 07.50 from Leeds on 18 May 1948.
J. C. Flemons

Right: No 35019 rests on arrival at Paddington on 20 April having headed an express from Plymouth. *C. C. B. Herbert*

Below: No 34004 *Yeovil* at Perth on 5 July 1948 on its preliminary run from there to Inverness. *G. L. Wilson*

Far right, top: No 34005 *Barnstaple,* sets out from St Pancras with a down Manchester train during the 1948 trials. *IAL*

Far right, bottom: No 34006 *Bude* backing out of Marylebone complete with the LNER Dynamometer car on 9 June 1948. *E. R. Wethersett/IAL*

9083
3
BRITISH
RAILWAYS

BRITISH
RAILWAYS
34006
SOUTHERN
34006
69804

2
The Preserved Bulleid Pacifics

Several of the Bulleid Pacifics, of both modified and unmodified varieties, have fortunately been purchased for preservation and restoration to running order. Some of then are already working trains, whilst others are still being stripped down and rebuilt.

Perhaps the most famous of these is rebuilt 'Merchant Navy' class No 35028 *Clan Line*, which has been working special trains over British Railways since 1974. *Clan Line* was one of the last few Pacifics to be withdrawn from service; one of a batch of seven in July 1967. Prior to its withdrawal, however, it was inspected by the Merchant Navy Locomotive Preservation Society and purchased by them on 10 July 1967. After a short sojourn at Nine Elms, it was moved to the Longmoor Military Railway, where members of the Society started restoring it. The engine was in steam again in October 1970; but before long the Longmoor Military Railway was closed, and attempts to purchase it privately failed. *Clan Line* accordingly had to be moved again, and the South Eastern Steam Society arranged to accommodate it at their depot in the Running Shed at Ashford. The task of restoring the engine to its pristine condition was completed at Ashford, and in 1973 British Railways authorised its use on steam tours over their system. The first of these was run between Basingstoke and Westbury on 27 April 1974. In 1975 *Clan Line* was among the distinguished steam locomotives present at Shildon to commemorate the 150th anniversary of the opening of the Stockton & Darlington Railway; and later that year it joined the Great Western No 6000 *King George V* at the Hereford depot of Messrs Bulmer.

In subsequent years *Clan Line* has been working a number of steam tours over British Railways, in conjunction with a few other steam locomotives which have passed the requisite BR tests. In 1979 BR asked the Society's permission for the engine to be left at York and be made available for their own steam-hauled excursions. This permission was granted and led to *Clan Line* covering a considerable mileage in the North of England.

Also in July 1967, No 34023 *Blackmore Vale*, the soundest of the unmodified Light Pacifics, was purchased by the Bulleid Preservation Society. It, too, travelled to the Longmoor Military Railway, where work was started on restoring it. Like *Clan Line*, it had to move on and in October 1971 it was transferred to the remarkable Bluebell Railway, where work on it was continued. On 15 May 1976 the engine was returned to traffic, bearing its old Bulleid number of 21C123 and painted in the Southern malachite green.

The Bluebell Railway was the earliest amateur operated standard gauge passenger railway in the world. It is a section of the old London Brighton & South Coast Railway line from East Grinstead to Lewes, lovingly nicknamed the 'Bluebell Line' and closed to all traffic on 16 March 1958. After long negotiations, the Bluebell Railway Preservation Society leased the five miles of single-line track from Sheffield Park to Horsted Keynes on 7 August 1960 and finally purchased it in 1967. Horsted Keynes station was originally excluded, but it was acquired after British Railways closed the branch between there and Haywards Heath. The Bluebell Railway Limited operates the line on behalf of the Preservation Society. *Blackmore Vale* joined the Bluebell's considerable stock of locomotives in operating the railway. All the locomotives are steam, and there are no plans to acquire any diesels.

Blackmore Vale was taken out of traffic in 1978 for a major overhaul by the Bluebell Railway's own very competent workshops staff, and was back in traffic for the season of 1979. No trouble has been experienced with the engine other than the familiar buckling of the cylinder drain cock operating rods. Steam-operated firedoors have worked satisfactorily and there has been no difficulty with the oil bath and valve gear, but the steam reversing gear has, as one would expect, been a little erratic. The trains are of course light and speeds very low.

In 1979 the Bluebell Railway bought a modified Light Pacific, No 34059 *Sir Archibald Sinclair*, which is the only 'Battle of Britain' version to be acquired for preservation. It was considered to be in better condition than any of the others still remaining at Woodham Brothers' Barry Island scrapyard. The engine is to be restored by the 'Bluebell Battle of Britain Locomotive Group'.

Another preserved line on which Bulleid Pacifics are running or being restored is the Mid-Hants Railway, which owns the stations of Alresford and Ropley and the three miles of single-line track between them. It is a section of the old London & South Western Railway 'Watercress Line' between Winchester and Alton. This was opened in 1865 as the Mid-Hants Railway and was not acquired by the LSWR until 1876. The Mid-Hants Railway Preservation Society is the supporting body of the officially named Winchester & Alton Railway Limited. The 10 miles of track bed between Ropley and Alton have also been purchased, and it is intended that the railway will eventually be extended to Alton. The Alresford-Ropley line was only re-opened on 30 April 1977, and the progress since then has been truly remarkable.

Of engines in traffic, the *pièce de résistance* is undoubtedly the rebuilt 'West Country' class No 34016 *Bodmin*. This locomotive was built in November 1945, rebuilt in July 1948, and withdrawn in June 1964. It then remained in the Barry scrapyard until privately purchased in 1972. On 29 July 1972 it was delivered at Quainton Road station, headquarters of the Quainton Railway Society, and a start was made on restoring it. In November 1976 it was moved to the Mid-

Hants Railway. In September 1979 work on the engine was finished and I was taken over it. The restoration had been beautifully done, with such attention to detail that *Bodmin* may well have been more pleasing to the eye than when originally rebuilt. The engine had been so named at Bodmin by the Mayor of the town in August 1946, being then, of course, in its unrebuilt condition and bearing its SR number 21C116. On 22 September 1979 it was renamed by the then Mayor of Bodmin at a ceremony at Alresford, attended too by the former Mayor who had performed the original naming. *Bodmin* then worked three special trains from Alresford to Ropley and return.

Another Bulleid Pacific is being restored at Ropley on the Mid-Hants Railway — the unrebuilt No 34105 *Swanage*, which arrived from Barry on 24 March 1978 in a condition that was described in the *Mid-Hants News* as 'not dissimilar to that of a rusty spam tin'. It looked much worse than it was because the air-smoothed casing has deteriorated badly in the South Wales sea air. In fact, it is one of the last batch of 'West Country' Pacifics, having been built in March 1950. It was withdrawn, after a short life, in October 1964, and had run not much more than 600,000 miles. The engine spent nearly all of those 14 years at Bournemouth, working trains to Waterloo and back, and over the Somerset & Dorset line. In 1951 it hauled the inaugural 'Royal Wessex' express from Weymouth to Waterloo. Perhaps, before too long, both *Bodmin* and *Swanage* will be seen at Alton.

At the time of writing there are a total of 15 Bulleid Pacifics preserved made up of the following:

'Merchant Navy'

35005 *Canadian Pacific* at Steamtown, Carnforth
35018 *British India Line* on the Mid-Hants Railway
35028 *Clan Line* at the Bulmer Railway Centre
35029 *Ellerman Lines* in the National Railway Museum

'Battle of Britain' & 'West Country'

34016 *Bodmin* on the Mid-Hants Railway
21C123 (34023) *Blackmore Vale* on the Bluebell Railway
34027 *Taw Valley* on the North Yorkshire Moors Railway
34039 *Boscastle* on the Great Central Railway
34051 *Winston Churchill* at the Didcot Railway Centre
34059 *Sir Archibald Sinclair* on the Bluebell Railway
34067 *Tangmere* on the Mid-Hants Railway
34081 *92 Squadron* on the Nene Valley Railway
34092 *City of Wells* on the Keighley & Worth Valley Railway
34101 *Hartland* under restoration in Derby
34105 *Swanage* on the Mid-Hants Railway

Below: 'Merchant Navy' No 35028 *Clan Line* is preserved at Hereford by the Merchant Navy Locomotive Preservation Society; No 35028 darkens the sky as she slips when backing down on to her train at Stratford-on-Avon in October 1974.
J. R. Woolley

THE MAYFLOWER
35028
10

34016

Left: ***Clan Line*** **nears Church Stretton with the return special from Chester to Hereford.** *R. E. B. Siviter*

Below left: 'West Country' No 34016 crosses the A31 road bridge outside Alresford on the Mid-Hants Railway where she was returned to service in August 1979.
K. A. Jaggers

Right: No 34016 now renamed ***Bodmin*** **on the first train of the day to Ropley.**
John Titlow

Below: 'West Country' No 21C123 ***Blackmore Vale*** **in May 1977 nears the top of Freshfield bank on the Bluebell Railway, where the Bulleid Society maintain her.**
P. Groom

Above: No 21C123 *Blackmore Vale* at the front of Freshfield bank in August 1977.
Brian Morrison

Right: At the time of writing the latest Bulleid Pacific to be returned to working order is 'West Country' No 34092 *City of Wells* on the Keighley & Worth Valley Railway, on 22 March 1980, an enthusiasts weekend, double-headed with the USA 2-8-0 No 5820 she makes a spirited departure from Keighley.
P. J. C. Skelton

Left: After the renaming ceremony on 1 April 1980, No 34092 *City of Wells* heads from Keighley complete with 'Golden Arrow' headboard.
J. Sagor

34092
34092

3
A List of the Bulleid Pacifics

'Merchant Navy' class

SR No	*BR No*	*Name*	*Built*	*Rebuilt*	*Withdrawn*
21C1	35001	*Channel Packet*	1941	1959	1964
21C2	35002	*Union Castle*	1941	1958	1964
21C3	35003	*Royal Mail*	1941	1959	1967
21C4	35004	*Cunard White Star*	1941	1958	1965
21C5	35005	*Canadian Pacific*	1941	1959	1965
21C6	35006	*Peninsular & Oriental SN Co*	1941	1959	1964
21C7	35007	*Aberdeen Commonwealth*	1942	1958	1967
21C8	35008	*Orient Line*	1942	1957	1967
21C9	35009	*Shaw Savill*	1942	1957	1964
21C10	35010	*Blue Star*	1942	1957	1966
21C11	35011	*General Steam Navigation*	1944	1959	1966
21C12	35012	*United States Lines*	1945	1957	1967
21C13	35013	*Blue Funnel*	1945	1956	1967
21C14	35014	*Nederland Line*	1945	1956	1967
21C15	35015	*Rotterdam Lloyd*	1945	1958	1964
21C16	35016	*Elders Fyffes*	1945	1957	1965
21C17	35017	*Belgian Marine*	1945	1957	1966
21C18	35018	*British India Line*	1945	1956	1964
21C19	35019	*French Line C.G.T.*	1945	1959	1965
21C20	35020	*Bibby Line*	1945	1956	1965
	35021	*New Zealand Line*	1945	1959	1965
	35022	*Holland Amerika Line*	1945	1956	1966
	35023	*Holland Afrika Line*	1945	1957	1967
	35024	*East Asiatic Company*	1948	1959	1965
	35025	*Brocklebank Line*	1948	1956	1964
	35026	*Lamport & Holt Line*	1948	1957	1967
	35027	*Port Line*	1948	1959	1966
	35028	*Clan Line*	1948	1959	1967
	35029	*Ellerman Lines*	1949	1959	1966
	35030	*Elder Dempster Lines*	1949	1958	1967

'West Country'/'Battle of Britain' class

SR No	*BR No*	*Name*	*Built*	*Rebuilt*	*Withdrawn*
21C101	34001	*Exeter*	1945	1957	1967
21C102	34002	*Salisbury*	1945		1967
21C103	34003	*Plymouth*	1945	1957	1964
21C104	34004	*Yeovil*	1945	1958	1967
21C105	34005	*Barnstaple*	1945	1957	1966
21C106	34006	*Bude*	1945		1967
21C107	34007	*Wadebridge*	1945		1965
21C108	34008	*Padstow*	1945	1960	1967
21C109	34009	*Lyme Regis*	1945	1961	1966
21C110	34010	*Sidmouth*	1945	1959	1965
21C111	34011	*Tavistock*	1945		1963
21C112	34012	*Launceston*	1945	1958	1966
21C113	34013	*Okehampton*	1945	1957	1967
21C114	34014	*Budleigh Salterton*	1945	1958	1965
21C115	34015	*Exmouth*	1945		1967
21C116	34016	*Bodmin*	1945	1958	1964

SR No	BR No	Name	Built	Rebuilt	Withdrawn
21C117	34017	*Ilfracombe*	1945	1957	1966
21C118	34018	*Axminster*	1945	1958	1967
21C119	34019	*Bideford*	1945		1967
21C120	34020	*Seaton*	1945		1964
21C121	34021	*Dartmoor*	1946	1958	1967
21C122	34022	*Exmoor*	1946	1957	1965
21C123	34023	*Blackmore Vale*	1946		1967
21C124	34024	*Tamar Valley*	1946	1961	1967
21C125	34025	*Whimple*	1946	1957	1967
21C126	34026	*Yes Tor*	1946	1958	1966
21C127	34027	*Taw Valley*	1946	1957	1964
21C128	34028	*Eddystone*	1946	1958	1964
21C129	34029	*Lundy*	1946	1958	1964
21C130	34030	*Watersmeet*	1946		1964
21C131	34031	*Torrington*	1946	1958	1965
21C132	34032	*Camelford*	1946	1960	1966
21C133	34033	*Chard*	1946		1965
21C134	34034	*Honiton*	1946	1960	1967
21C135	34035	*Shaftesbury*	1946		1963
21C136	34036	*Westward Ho!*	1946	1960	1967
21C137	34037	*Clovelly*	1946	1958	1967
21C138	34038	*Lynton*	1946		1966
21C139	34039	*Boscastle*	1946	1959	1965
21C140	34040	*Crewkerne*	1946	1960	1967
21C141	34041	*Wilton*	1946		1966
21C142	34042	*Dorchester*	1946	1959	1965
21C143	34043	*Combe Martin*	1946		1963
21C144	34044	*Woolacombe*	1946	1960	1967
21C145	34045	*Ottery St Mary*	1946	1958	1964
21C146	34046	*Braunton*	1946	1959	1965
21C147	34047	*Callington*	1946	1958	1967
21C148	34048	*Crediton*	1946	1959	1966
21C149	34049	*Anti-Aircraft Command*	1946		1963
21C150	34050	*Royal Observer Corps*	1946	1958	1965
21C151	34051	*Winston Churchill*	1946		1965
21C152	34052	*Lord Dowding*	1946	1958	1967
21C153	34053	*Sir Keith Park*	1947	1958	1965
21C154	34054	*Lord Beaverbrook*	1947		1964
21C155	34055	*Fighter Pilot*	1947		1963
21C156	34056	*Croydon*	1947	1960	1967
21C157	34057	*Biggin Hill*	1947		1967
21C158	34058	*Sir Frederick Pile*	1947	1960	1964
21C159	34059	*Sir Archibald Sinclair*	1947	1960	1966
21C160	34060	*25 Squadron*	1947	1960	1967
21C161	34061	*73 Squadron*	1947		1964
21C162	34062	*17 Squadron*	1947	1959	1964
21C163	34063	*229 Squadron*	1947		1965
21C164	34064	*Fighter Command*	1947		1966
21C165	34065	*Hurricane*	1947		1964
21C166	34066	*Spitfire*	1947		1966
21C167	34067	*Tangmere*	1947		1963
21C168	34068	*Kenley*	1947		1963
21C169	34069	*Hawkinge*	1947		1963
21C170	34070	*Manston*	1947		1964
	34071	*601 Squadron*	1948	1960	1967
	34072	*257 Squadron*	1948		1964
	34073	*249 Squadron*	1948		1964
	34074	*46 Squadron*	1948		1963
	34075	*264 Squadron*	1948		1964
	34076	*41 Squadron*	1948		1966
	34077	*603 Squadron*	1948	1960	1967
	34078	*222 Squadron*	1948		1964
	34079	*141 Squadron*	1948		1966

SR No	BR No	Name	Built	Rebuilt	Withdrawn
	34080	*74 Squadron*	1948		1964
	34081	*92 Squadron*	1948		1964
	34082	*615 Squadron*	1948	1960	1966
	34083	*605 Squadron*	1948		1964
	34084	*253 Squadron*	1948		1965
	34085	*501 Squadron*	1948	1960	1965
	34086	*219 Squadron*	1948		1966
	34087	*145 Squadron*	1948	1960	1967
	34088	*213 Squadron*	1948	1960	1967
	34089	*602 Squadron*	1948	1960	1967
	34090	*Sir Eustace Missenden Southern Railway*	1949	1960	1967
	34091	*Weymouth*	1949		1964
	34092	*City of Wells*	1949		1964
	34093	*Saunton*	1949	1960	1967
	34094	*Mortehoe*	1949		1964
	34095	*Brentor*	1949	1961	1967
	34096	*Trevone*	1949	1961	1964
	34097	*Holsworthy*	1949	1961	1966
	34098	*Templecombe*	1949	1961	1967
	34099	*Lynmouth*	1949		1964
	34100	*Appledore*	1949	1960	1967
	34101	*Hartland*	1950	1960	1966
	34102	*Lapford*	1950		1967
	34103	*Calstock*	1950		1965
	34104	*Bere Alston*	1950	1961	1967
	34105	*Swanage*	1950		1964
	34106	*Lydford*	1950		1964
	34107	*Blandford Forum*	1950		1964
	34108	*Wincanton*	1950	1961	1967
	34109	*Sir Trafford Leigh-Mallory*	1950	1961	1964
	34110	*66 Squadron*	1951		1963

Below: With a stopping train for Padstow, No 34017 *Ilfracombe* leaves Wadebridge station.
B. A. Butt

Index